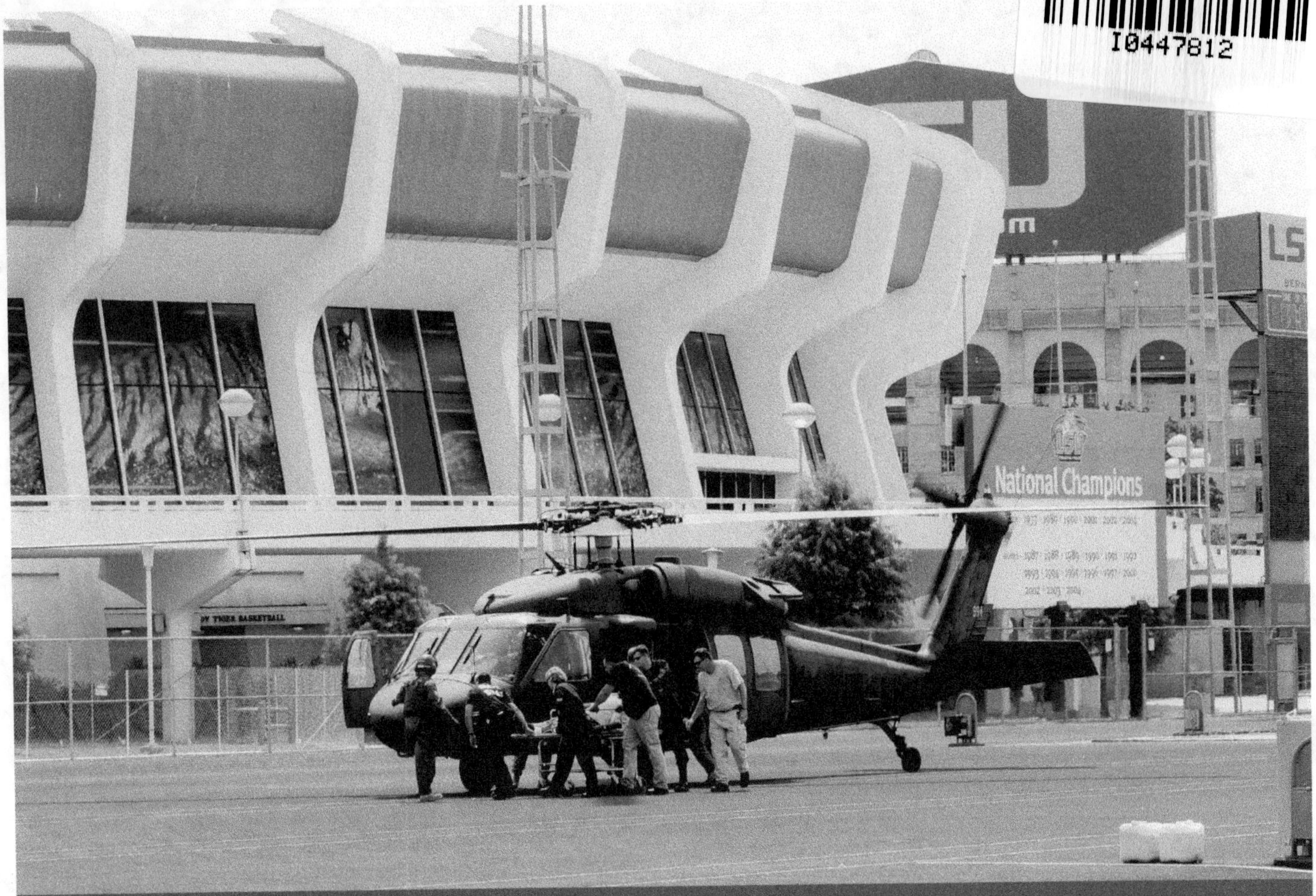

IS-100.HE:
Introduction to the Incident Command System, ICS-100 for Higher Education

Instructor Guide

November 2008

FEMA

ICS-100: Introduction to ICS for Higher Education

Instructor Guide

November 2008

Purpose   This course provides training on and resources for personnel who require a basic understanding of the Incident Command System (ICS).

Who Should Attend   ICS-100, Introduction to the Incident Command System for Higher Education Institutions, introduces the Incident Command System (ICS) and provides the foundation for higher level ICS training. This course describes the history, features and principles, and organizational structure of the Incident Command System. It also explains the relationship between ICS and the National Incident Management System (NIMS).

The target audience includes persons involved with emergency planning, response, and/or recovery efforts on campus.

ICS Instructor Guidelines   The FEMA National Integration Center (NIC) Incident Management Systems Integration Division is responsible for facilitating the development of national guidelines for incident management training and exercises at all jurisdictional levels. This document provides guidelines for ICS instructors.

While individual agencies and organizations are responsible for establishing and certifying instructors, the NIC urges those agencies and organizations to follow these guidelines.

The NIC recommends the following ICS general instructor guidelines:

Instructor Levels

- <u>Lead instructors</u> must have sufficient experience in presenting all units of the course so they are capable of last-minute substitution for unit instructors.

- <u>Unit instructors</u> must be experienced in the lesson content they are presenting.

- <u>Adjunct instructors</u> may provide limited instruction in specialized knowledge and skills at the discretion of the lead instructor. They must be experienced, proficient, and knowledgeable of current issues in their field of expertise.

Training Requirements for Lead and Unit Instructors

Instructors should have formal instructor training (NWCG Facilitative Instructor, M-410, EMI Master Trainer Program, Office for Domestic Preparedness Instructor Course, or equivalent).

ICS-100 Instructor Qualifications

It is recommended that this training be team taught by instructors with the following minimum qualifications:

- One instructor required, two recommended.

- Lead and Unit instructors successfully completed ICS-100, ICS-200, and EMI's IS-700 (NIMS: An Introduction).

- Lead instructor should have served as Incident Commander, or on Command or General Staff in five incidents.

Course Objective

The course objective is to enable participants to demonstrate basic knowledge of the Incident Command System (ICS).

Training Content

The training is comprised of the following units:

- Unit 1: Course Overview
- Unit 2: ICS Overview
- Unit 3: ICS Features and Principles
- Unit 4: Incident Commander & Command Staff Functions
- Unit 5: General Staff Functions
- Unit 6: Unified Command
- Unit 7: Course Summary – Putting It All Together

The below table presents the recommended training agenda.

Morning Session	Unit 1: Course Overview	35 minutes
	Unit 2: ICS Overview	1 hour
	Unit 3: ICS Features and Principles	1 hour 45 minutes
Afternoon Session	Unit 4: Incident Commander & Command Staff Functions	1 hour
	Unit 5: General Staff Functions	1 hour 45 minutes
	Unit 6: Unified Command	55 minutes
	Unit 7: Course Summary – Putting It All Together	1 hour 15 minutes

ICS Training and NIMS

The National Incident Management Systems (NIMS) National Standard Curriculum: Training Development Guidance outlines the system's ICS concepts and principles, management characteristics, organizations and operations, organizational element titles, and recommendations for a model curriculum. It also provides an evaluation checklist for content that may be used to make sure that the training meets the "as taught by DHS" standard. The guidance document is available for download from the NIMS Homepage at http://www.fema.gov/emergency/nims.

The model NIMS ICS curriculum organizes four levels of training: ICS-100, Introduction to ICS; ICS-200, Basic ICS; ICS-300, Intermediate ICS; and ICS-400, Advanced ICS. ICS training provided by the Emergency Management Institute (EMI), the National Fire Academy (NFA), the National Wildfire Coordinating Group (NWCG), the U.S. Department of Agriculture (USDA), the Environmental Protection Agency (EPA), and the U.S. Coast Guard (USCG) follows this model.

According to the FEMA National Integration Center (NIC) Incident Management Systems Integration Division, emergency management and response personnel already ICS trained do not need retraining if their previous training is consistent with the DHS standard. Acceptable ICS training would include ICS courses managed, administered, or delivered by EMI, NFA, NWCG, USDA, EPA, or USCG. For more information about NIMS ICS, go to http://www.fema.gov/emergency/nims/.

Course Logistics Overview

Course Materials

Listed below are the materials that you will need in order to conduct this course:

- **Instructor Guide and Resource CD:** Obtain one copy of the Instructor Guide and resource CD for each trainer.

- **Student Manual:** Secure one copy of the Student Manual for each person attending the session.

- **PowerPoint Files CD:** The course visuals and videos are stored on a CD. **Transfer the course visuals from the CD to the hard drive of a computer.** The visuals and videos will operate more effectively if they are accessed from the computer's hard drive instead of the CD. Complete the following steps for copying the folders and files from the CD:
  1. Insert the Visuals CD in your CD drive.
  2. Using Windows Explorer, access the list of folders and files on your CD drive.
  3. Highlight the folder on the CD titled "visuals."
  4. With the visual folder highlighted, click on the Edit pull-down menu and then select Copy.
  5. Select a location on your computer's hard drive. When you are in that drive (and folder), click on the Edit pull-down menu and then select Paste.
  6. All of the visuals and videos should now be copied onto your hard drive. It is important to copy the entire main visual folder rather than the individual files. This method will ensure that the videos stay linked to the visuals!
  7. Test the visuals and videos to make sure that everything transferred correctly. Remember that the videos will only play when you are in the "Slide Show" mode.

- **Course Evaluation Forms:** Make sure that you have one copy of the course evaluation form for each person attending the training.

Course Equipment

The following equipment is required for conducting this course:

- **Computer and Projection Device:** Make arrangements to have a computer with a PowerPoint slide projector. Be sure to try out the projector in advance of the training, in case you need help getting it to work properly. Make sure all equipment is functioning properly. Test the PowerPoint projector and the lights. If you do not have equipment for projection, plan to refer participants to their Student Manuals. The visuals are reproduced in the Student Manual, but the training is more effective with the projection of the visuals. Arrange for technical assistance to be available during training in the event of equipment malfunction.

- **Speakers or Output to a Sound System:** The speakers built into a typical computer will not be loud enough for the audience to hear the audio elements within the digital video segments.

Copyright

This course makes no use of copyrighted/proprietary material.

Unit 1: Course Overview

Objectives

At the end of this unit, the participants should be able to describe the purpose of the course.

Scope

- Unit Introduction
- Course Objective
- Participant Introductions
- Expectations: Participant and Instructor
- Course Structure
- Course Logistics
- Successful Course Completion

Methodology

The instructors will welcome the participants to the course and introduce themselves. They will also review the course objective and show a brief video that illustrates the importance of ICS for higher education. Following instructor introductions, each participant will introduce himself or herself to the rest of the group. After introductions, the instructors will facilitate a discussion about what the group expects to gain from the course.

The instructors will then provide guidelines for the behavior they expect from each participant. The instructors will also explain the course structure and logistics. Finally, they will describe what is required for successful course completion. The instructors will then transition to Unit 2, which provides an overview of the Incident Command System (ICS).

Time Plan

A suggested time plan for this unit is shown below. More or less time may be required, based on the experience level of the group.

Topic	Time
Unit Introduction and Course Objective	5 minutes
Introductions and Expectations	20 minutes
Course Structure and Logistics	5 minutes
Successful Course Completion	5 minutes
Total Time	**35 minutes**

This page intentionally left blank.

Topic	Unit Introduction

Visual 1.1

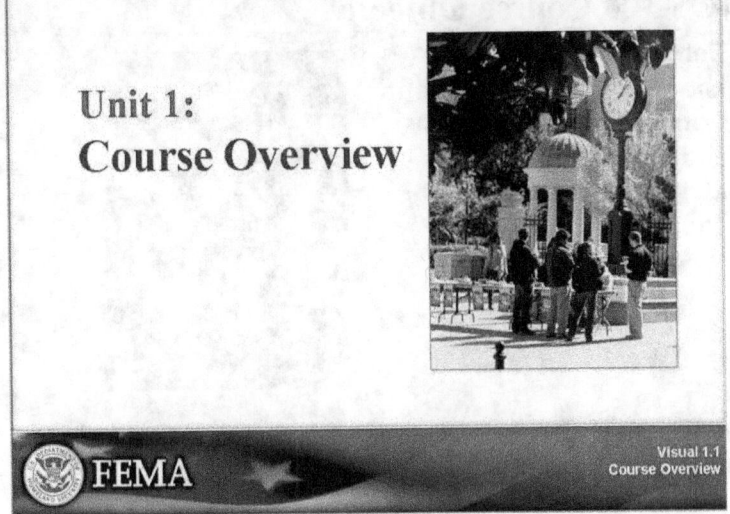

Visual Description: Unit Introduction

Instructor Notes

Welcome the participants to the course.

Tell the participants that this course will introduce them to the Incident Command System (ICS).

Introduce yourself by providing:

- Your name and organization.
- A brief statement of your experience with emergency or incident response using ICS, and your experience with incidents.

| Topic | ICS-100 Course Objective |

Visual 1.2

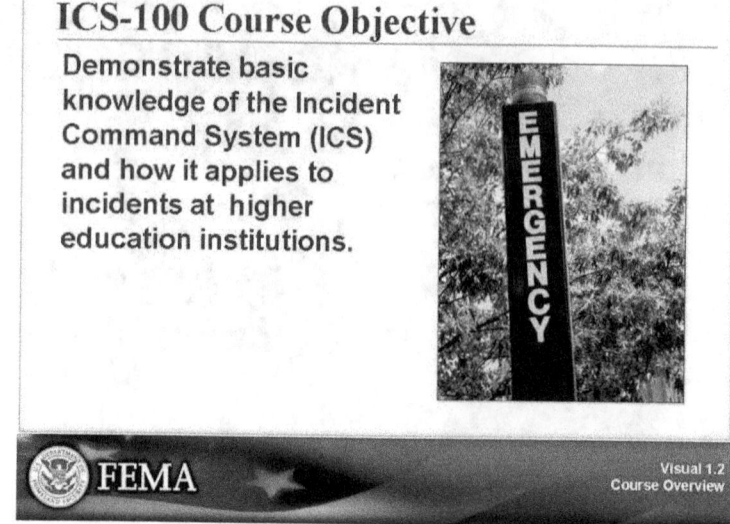

Visual Description: ICS-100 Course Objective

Instructor Notes

Tell participants that the objective for this course is for participants to demonstrate basic knowledge of the Incident Command System (ICS) and how ICS applies to higher education.

Tell the participants that this course is designed to provide overall incident management skills rather than tactical expertise. Additional courses are available on developing and implementing incident tactics.

Explain that the brief video you are going to show will provide an overview of the purpose and objective of this course.

| Topic | Video: ICS: Promoting Safer Higher Education Settings |

Visual 1.3

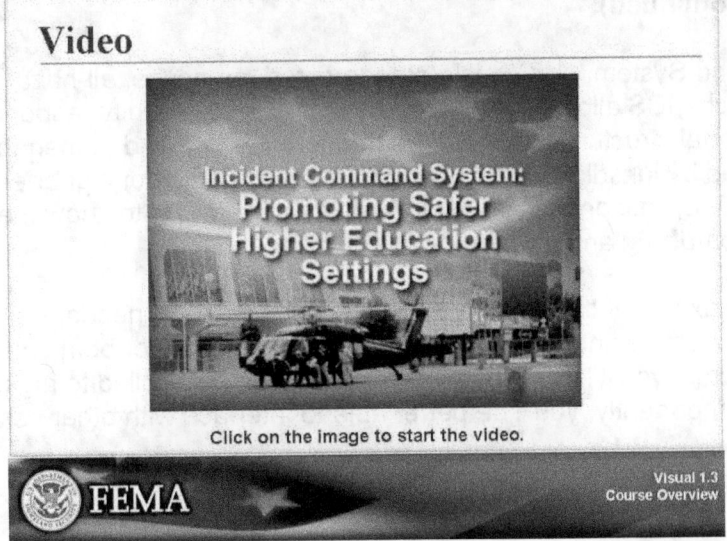

Visual Description: Video: Incident Command System: Promoting Safer Higher Education Settings

Instructor Notes

Tell the participants that this brief (2-minute) video presents a review of the purpose of ICS.

Instructions for playing videos: The videos are activated by a single click on the image in Slide Show mode. If you click a second time on the video, it will stop. The videos will not work unless you are in Slide Show mode.

Video Transcript:

Each year, natural disasters such as tornadoes, floods, and severe storms affect our communities. Health-related incidents such as flu outbreaks, food-borne diseases, and even rabid animals can threaten all of us. Unfortunately, institutes of higher education are not immune from these threats and others, such as intruders, crime, and violence. And accidents, whether in research labs, sporting venues, or on campus shuttles, may occur.

When Hurricane Katrina struck the gulf coast in 2005, the University of Southern Mississippi incurred an estimated $57 million, and the storm cost Tulane University more than $200 million in damages. Higher education institutes across the region were affected, not just by the structural damages, but also by setbacks in their scientific research and medical developments.

Given today's threats, higher education institutions must be prepared to respond in partnership with local, State, tribal, and Federal agencies. As partners, you must respond together in a seamless, coordinated fashion using the same terminology and approach.

(Continued on next page.)

Video Transcript (Continued):

The Incident Command System, or ICS, is a standardized, on-scene, all-hazard incident management approach. ICS allows campus personnel and community responders to adopt an integrated organizational structure that matches the complexities and demands of the incidents without being hindered by jurisdictional boundaries. With institutes of higher education blending into the larger community response system, ICS allows all involved to know their roles and work together, without jeopardizing anyone's voice or authority.

The ICS structure is flexible. It can grow or shrink to meet different needs. This flexibility makes it a very cost-effective and efficient management approach for both small and large situations. In this course, you'll learn ICS principles that can be applied to higher education settings. And, more importantly, you'll be better able to interface with other community responders.

Topic	Participant Introductions

Visual 1.4

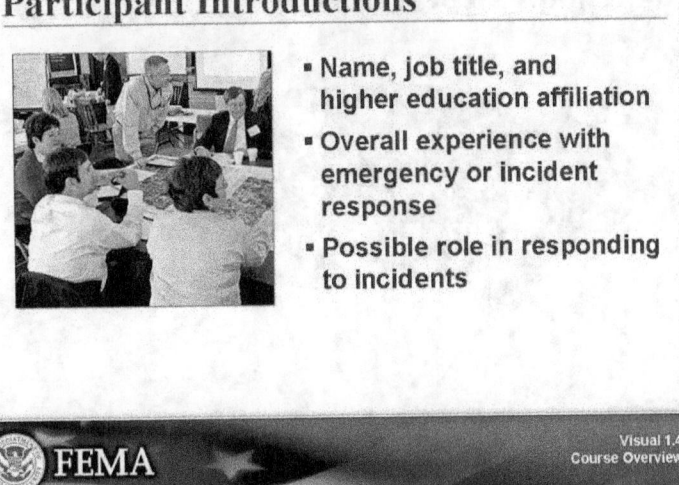

Visual Description: Participant Introductions

Instructor Notes

Ask the participants to introduce themselves by providing:

- Their names, job titles, and higher education affiliations.

- A brief statement of their overall experience with emergency or incident response.

- Their possible roles in responding to incidents.

Instructor Note: Some participants may not know what their role would be during an incident. Explain that this may be a simple as following instructions.

| Topic | Participant Expectations |

Visual 1.5

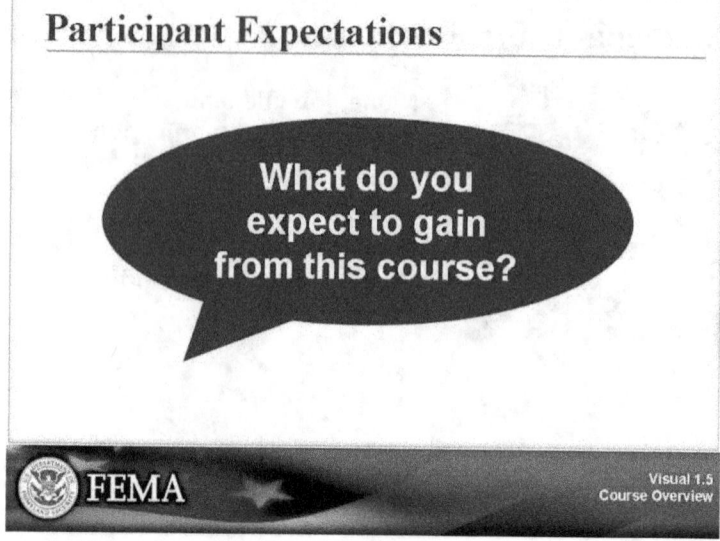

Visual Description: Participant Expectations: What do you expect to gain from this course?

Instructor Notes

Ask the participants the following question:

What do you expect to gain from this course?

Allow the group time to respond.

Record their responses on chart paper.

If possible, hang the list of their responses in the training room. Revisit the list at the end of the course to ensure that participants have met their learning objectives.

Topic	**Instructor Expectations**

Visual 1.6

Instructor Expectations

- Cooperate with the group.
- Be open minded to new ideas.
- Participate actively in all of the training activities and exercises.
- Return to class at the stated time.
- Use what you learn in the course to perform effectively within an ICS organization.

FEMA

Visual 1.6
Course Overview

Visual Description: Instructor Expectations

Instructor Notes

Explain that like the participants, you, as the instructor, also have expectations for the course. You expect that everyone will:

- Cooperate with the group.
- Be open minded to new ideas.
- Participate actively in all of the training activities and exercises.
- Return to class at the stated time.
- Use what they learn in the course to perform effectively within an ICS organization.

Topic | **Course Structure**

Visual 1.7

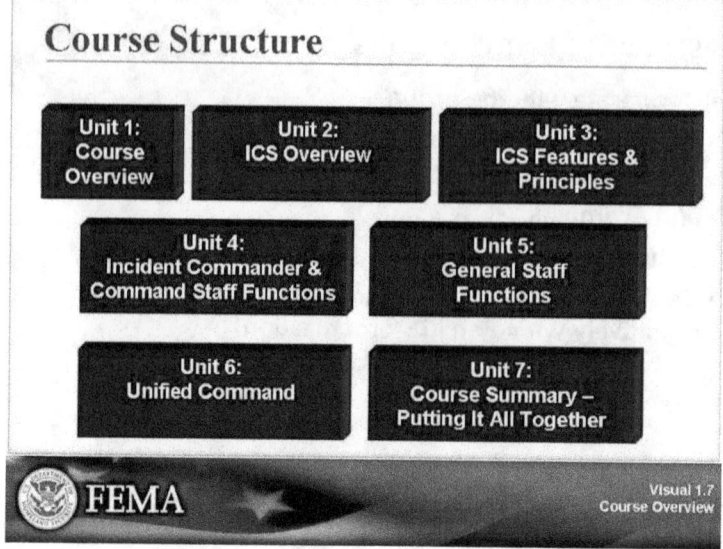

Visual Description: Course Structure – Unit 1: Course Overview; Unit 2: ICS Overview; Unit 3: ICS Features and Principles; Unit 4: Incident Commander & Command Staff Functions; Unit 5: General Staff Functions; Unit 6: Unified Command; Unit 7: Course Summary – Putting It All Together

Instructor Notes

Tell participants that the course is divided into the following seven units:

- Unit 1: Course Overview
- Unit 2: ICS Overview
- Unit 3: ICS Features and Principles
- Unit 4: Incident Commander & Command Staff Functions
- Unit 5: General Staff Functions
- Unit 6: Unified Command
- Unit 7: Course Summary – Putting It All Together

Topic	Course Logistics

Visual 1.8

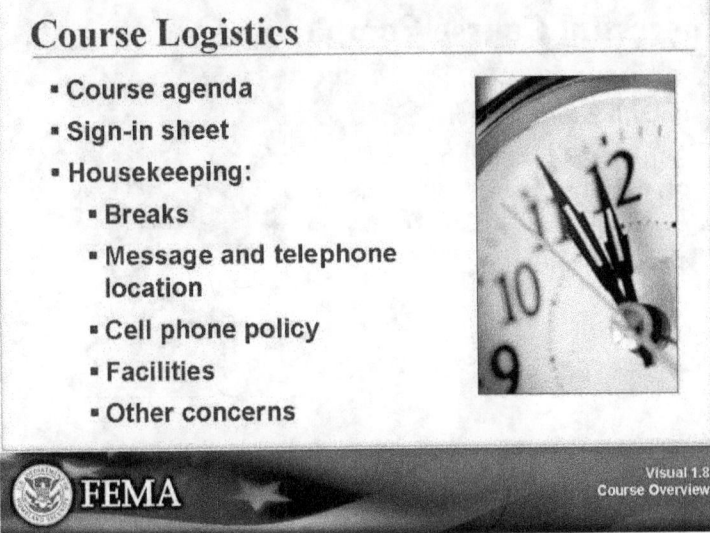

Visual Description: Course Logistics

Instructor Notes

Review the following information with the group:

- Course agenda
- Sign-in sheet

Review the following housekeeping issues:

- Breaks
- Message and telephone location
- Cell phone policy
- Facilities
- Other concerns

Instructor Note: Tell participants that the course glossary is located at the end of this unit, and they should use it throughout the course. Note that some of the terms in the glossary may be used differently in ICS than in day-to-day operations on campus (e.g., facilities).

| Topic | Successful Course Completion |

Visual 1.9

Successful Course Completion

- Participate in unit activities/exercises.
- Achieve 75% or higher on the final exam.
- Complete the end-of-course evaluation.

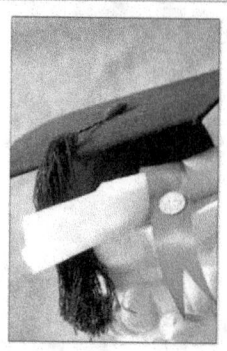

FEMA

Visual 1.9
Course Overview

Visual Description: Successful Course Completion

Instructor Notes

Tell participants that in order to successfully complete this course, they must:

- Participate in unit activities/exercises.
- Achieve 75% or higher on the final exam.
- Complete the end-of-course evaluation.

Ask if anyone has any questions about anything covered in this unit.

Explain that the next unit will provide an overview of the Incident Command System.

Refer the participants to the glossary located at the end of this unit. Encourage participants to refer to this glossary throughout the training session.

ICS 100: Introduction to ICS for Higher Education Institutions
Sample Agenda

DAY ONE

Morning Session

- Unit 1: Course Overview (35 minutes)
- Unit 2: ICS Overview (1 hour)
- Unit 3: ICS Features and Principles (1 hour 45 minutes)

Afternoon Session

- Unit 4: Incident Commander & Command Staff Functions (1 hour)
- Unit 5: General Staff Functions (1 hour 45 minutes)
- Unit 6: Unified Command (55 minutes)
- Unit 7: Course Summary – Putting It All Together (1 hour 15 minutes)

Your Notes:

A

Action Plan: See Incident Action Plan.

Agency: An agency is a division of government with a specific function, or a nongovernmental organization (e.g., private contractor, business, etc.) that offers a particular kind of assistance. In ICS, agencies are defined as jurisdictional (having statutory responsibility for incident mitigation) or assisting and/or cooperating (providing resources and/or assistance). (See Assisting Agency, Cooperating Agency, Jurisdictional Agency, and Multiagency Incident.)

Agency Administrator or Executive: Chief executive officer (or designee) of the agency or jurisdiction that has responsibility for the incident.

Agency Dispatch: The agency or jurisdictional facility from which resources are allocated to incidents.

Agency Representative: An individual assigned to an incident from an assisting or cooperating agency who has been delegated authority to make decisions on matters affecting that agency's participation at the incident. Agency Representatives report to the Incident Liaison Officer.

Air Operations Branch Director: The person primarily responsible for preparing and implementing the air operations portion of the Incident Action Plan. Also responsible for providing logistical support to helicopters operating on the incident.

Allocated Resources: Resources dispatched to an incident.

All-Risk: Any incident or event, natural or human-caused, that warrants action to protect life, property, the environment, and public health and safety, and minimize disruption of governmental, social, and economic activities.

Area Command (Unified Area Command): An organization established to oversee the management of (1) multiple incidents that are each being handled by an ICS organization, or (2) large or multiple incidents to which several Incident Management Teams have been assigned. Area Command has the responsibility to set overall strategy and priorities, allocate critical resources according to priorities, ensure that incidents are properly managed, and ensure that objectives are met and strategies followed. Area Command becomes Unified Area Command when incidents are multijurisdictional. Area Command may be established at an emergency operations center facility or at some location other than an Incident Command Post.

Assigned Resources: Resources checked in and assigned work tasks on an incident.

Assignments: Tasks given to resources to perform within a given operational period, based upon tactical objectives in the Incident Action Plan.

Assistant: Title for subordinates of the Command Staff positions. The title indicates a level of technical capability, qualifications, and responsibility subordinate to the primary positions.

Assisting Agency: An agency or organization providing personnel, services, or other resources to the agency with direct responsibility for incident management.

Available Resources: Resources assigned to an incident, checked in, and available for a mission assignment, normally located in a Staging Area.

B

Base: The location at which primary Logistics functions for an incident are coordinated and administered. There is only one Base per incident. (Incident name or other designator will be added to the term Base.) The Incident Command Post may be collocated with the Base.

Branch: The organizational level having functional or geographic responsibility for major parts of the Operations or Logistics functions. The Branch level is organizationally between Section and Division/Group in the Operations Section, and between Section and Units in the Logistics Section. Branches are identified by the use of Roman numerals or by functional name (e.g., medical, security, etc.).

C

Cache: A pre-determined complement of tools, equipment, and/or supplies stored in a designated location, available for incident use.

Camp: A geographical site, within the general incident area, separate from the Incident Base, equipped and staffed to provide sleeping, food, water, and sanitary services to incident personnel.

Chain of Command: A series of management positions in order of authority.

Check-In: The process whereby resources first report to an incident. Check-in locations include: Incident Command Post (Resources Unit), Incident Base, Camps, Staging Areas, Helibases, Helispots, and Division Supervisors (for direct line assignments).

Chief: The ICS title for individuals responsible for functional Sections: Operations, Planning, Logistics, and Finance/Administration.

Clear Text: The use of plain English in radio communications transmissions. No Ten Codes or agency-specific codes are used when utilizing clear text.

Command: The act of directing and/or controlling resources by virtue of explicit legal, agency, or delegated authority. May also refer to the Incident Commander.

Command Post: See Incident Command Post.

Command Staff: The Command Staff consists of the Public Information Officer, Safety Officer, and Liaison Officer. They report directly to the Incident Commander. They may have an Assistant or Assistants, as needed.

Communications Unit: An organizational Unit in the Logistics Section responsible for providing communication services at an incident. A Communications Unit may also be a facility (e.g., a trailer or mobile van) used to provide the major part of an Incident Communications Center.

Compacts: Formal working agreements among agencies to obtain mutual aid.

Compensation/Claims Unit: Functional Unit within the Finance/Administration Section responsible for financial concerns resulting from property damage, injuries, or fatalities at the incident.

Complex: Two or more individual incidents located in the same general area that are assigned to a single Incident Commander or to Unified Command.

Cooperating Agency: An agency supplying assistance other than direct operational or support functions or resources to the incident management effort.

Coordination: The process of systematically analyzing a situation, developing relevant information, and informing appropriate command authority of viable alternatives for selection of the most effective combination of available resources to meet specific objectives. The coordination process (which can be either intra- or interagency) does not involve dispatch actions. However, personnel responsible for coordination may perform command or dispatch functions within the limits established by specific agency delegations, procedures, legal authority, etc.

Coordination Center: A facility that is used for the coordination of agency or jurisdictional resources in support of one or more incidents.

Cost-Sharing Agreements: Agreements between agencies or jurisdictions to share designated costs related to incidents. Cost-sharing agreements are normally written but may also be oral between authorized agency or jurisdictional representatives at the incident.

Cost Unit: Functional Unit within the Finance/Administration Section responsible for tracking costs, analyzing cost data, making cost estimates, and recommending cost-saving measures.

Crew: See Single Resource.

D

Delegation of Authority: A statement provided to the Incident Commander by the Agency Executive delegating authority and assigning responsibility. The Delegation of Authority can include objectives, priorities, expectations, constraints, and other considerations or guidelines as needed. Many agencies require written Delegation of Authority to be given to Incident Commanders prior to their assuming command on larger incidents.

Demobilization Unit: Functional Unit within the Planning Section responsible for assuring orderly, safe, and efficient demobilization of incident resources.

Deputy: A fully qualified individual who, in the absence of a superior, could be delegated the authority to manage a functional operation or perform a specific task. In some cases, a Deputy could act as relief for a superior and therefore must be fully qualified in the position. Deputies can be assigned to the Incident Commander, General Staff, and Branch Directors.

Director: The ICS title for individuals responsible for supervision of a Branch.

Dispatch: The implementation of a command decision to move a resource or resources from one place to another.

Dispatch Center: A facility from which resources are ordered, mobilized, and assigned to an incident.

Division: Divisions are used to divide an incident into geographical areas of operation. A Division is located within the ICS organization between the Branch and the Task Force/Strike Team. (See Group.) Divisions are identified by alphabetic characters for horizontal applications and, often, by floor numbers when used in buildings.

Documentation Unit: Functional Unit within the Planning Section responsible for collecting, recording, and safeguarding all documents relevant to the incident.

E

Emergency: Absent a Presidentially declared emergency, any incident(s), human-caused or natural, that requires responsive action to protect life or property. Under the Robert T. Stafford Disaster Relief and Emergency Assistance Act, an emergency means any occasion or instance for which, in the determination of the President, Federal assistance is needed to supplement State and local efforts and capabilities to save lives and to protect property and public health and safety, or to lessen or avert the threat of a catastrophe in any part of the United States.

Emergency Management Coordinator/Director: The individual within each institution that has coordination responsibility for jurisdictional emergency management.

Emergency Operations Centers (EOCs): The physical location at which the coordination of information and resources to support domestic incident management activities normally takes place. An EOC may be a temporary facility or may be located in a more central or permanently established facility, perhaps at a higher level of organization within a jurisdiction. EOCs may be organized by major functional disciplines (e.g., fire, law enforcement, and medical services), by jurisdiction (e.g., Federal, State, regional, county, city, tribal), or some combination thereof.

Emergency Operations Plan (EOP): The plan that each jurisdiction has and maintains for responding to appropriate hazards.

Event: A planned, non-emergency activity. ICS can be used as the management system for a wide range of events, e.g., parades, concerts, or sporting events.

F

Facilities Unit: Functional Unit within the Support Branch of the Logistics Section that provides fixed facilities for the incident. These facilities may include the Incident Base, feeding areas, sleeping areas, sanitary facilities, etc.

Federal: Of or pertaining to the Federal Government of the United States of America.

Field Operations Guide: A pocket-size manual of instructions on the application of the Incident Command System.

Finance/Administration Section: The Section responsible for all incident costs and financial considerations. Includes the Time Unit, Procurement Unit, Compensation/Claims Unit, and Cost Unit.

Food Unit: Functional Unit within the Service Branch of the Logistics Section responsible for providing meals for incident personnel.

Function: Function refers to the five major activities in ICS: Command, Operations, Planning, Logistics, and Finance/Administration. The term function is also used when describing the activity involved, e.g., the planning function. A sixth function, Intelligence, may be established, if required, to meet incident management needs.

G

General Staff: A group of incident management personnel organized according to function and reporting to the Incident Commander. The General Staff normally consists of the Operations Section Chief, Planning Section Chief, Logistics Section Chief, and Finance/Administration Section Chief.

Ground Support Unit: Functional Unit within the Support Branch of the Logistics Section responsible for the fueling, maintaining, and repairing of vehicles, and the transportation of personnel and supplies.

Group: Groups are established to divide the incident into functional areas of operation. Groups are composed of resources assembled to perform a special function not necessarily within a single geographic division. (See Division.) Groups are located between Branches (when activated) and Resources in the Operations Section.

H

Hazard: Something that is potentially dangerous or harmful, often the root cause of an unwanted outcome.

Helibase: The main location for parking, fueling, maintenance, and loading of helicopters operating in support of an incident. It is usually located at or near the incident Base.

Helispot: Any designated location where a helicopter can safely take off and land. Some Helispots may be used for loading of supplies, equipment, or personnel.

Hierarchy of Command: See Chain of Command.

I

Incident: An occurrence or event, natural or human-caused, that requires an emergency response to protect life or property. Incidents can, for example, include major disasters, emergencies, terrorist attacks, terrorist threats, wildland and urban fires, floods, hazardous materials spills, nuclear accidents, aircraft accidents, earthquakes, hurricanes, tornadoes, tropical storms, war-related disasters, public health and medical emergencies, and other occurrences requiring an emergency response.

Incident Action Plan (IAP): An oral or written plan containing general objectives reflecting the overall strategy for managing an incident. It may include the identification of operational resources and assignments. It may also include attachments that provide direction and important information for management of the incident during one or more operational periods.

Incident Base: Location at the incident where the primary Logistics functions are coordinated and administered. (Incident name or other designator will be added to the term Base.) The Incident Command Post may be collocated with the Base. There is only one Base per incident.

Incident Commander (IC): The individual responsible for all incident activities, including the development of strategies and tactics and the ordering and the release of resources. The IC has overall authority and responsibility for conducting incident operations and is responsible for the management of all incident operations at the incident site.

Incident Command Post (ICP): The field location at which the primary tactical-level, on-scene incident command functions are performed. The ICP may be collocated with the incident Base or other incident facilities and is normally identified by a green rotating or flashing light.

Incident Command System (ICS): A standardized on-scene emergency management construct specifically designed to provide for the adoption of an integrated organizational structure that reflects the complexity and demands of single or multiple incidents, without being hindered by jurisdictional boundaries. ICS is the combination of facilities, equipment, personnel, procedures, and communications operating within a common organizational structure, designed to aid in the management of resources during incidents. It is used for all kinds of emergencies and is applicable to small as well as large and complex incidents. ICS is used by various jurisdictions and functional agencies, both public and private, to organize field-level incident management operations.

Incident Communications Center: The location of the Communications Unit and the Message Center.

Incident Complex: See Complex.

Incident Management Team (IMT): The Incident Commander and appropriate Command and General Staff personnel assigned to an incident.

Incident Objectives: Statements of guidance and direction necessary for the selection of appropriate strategy(ies), and the tactical direction of resources. Incident objectives are based on realistic expectations of what can be accomplished when all allocated resources have been effectively deployed. Incident objectives must be achievable and measurable, yet flexible enough to allow for strategic and tactical alternatives.

Incident Types: Incidents are categorized by five types based on complexity. Type 5 incidents are the least complex and Type 1 the most complex.

Incident Support Organization: Includes any off-incident support provided to an incident. Examples would be Agency Dispatch Centers, Airports, Mobilization Centers, etc.

Initial Action: The actions taken by resources that are the first to arrive at an incident site.

Initial Response: Resources initially committed to an incident.

Intelligence Officer: The intelligence officer is responsible for managing internal information, intelligence, and operational security requirements supporting incident management activities. These may include information security and operational security activities, as well as the complex task of ensuring that sensitive information of all types (e.g., classified information, law enforcement sensitive information, proprietary information, or export-controlled information) is handled in a way that not only safeguards the information, but also ensures that it gets to those who need access to it to perform their missions effectively and safely.

J

Joint Information Center (JIC): A facility established to coordinate all incident-related public information activities. It is the central point of contact for all news media at the scene of the incident. Public information officials from all participating agencies should collocate at the JIC.

Joint Information System (JIS): Integrates incident information and public affairs into a cohesive organization designed to provide consistent, coordinated, timely information during crisis or incident operations. The mission of the JIS is to provide a structure and system for developing and delivering coordinated interagency messages; developing, recommending, and executing public information plans and strategies on behalf of the Incident Commander; advising the Incident Commander concerning public affairs issues that could affect a response effort; and controlling rumors and inaccurate information that could undermine public confidence in the emergency response effort.

Jurisdiction: A range or sphere of authority. Public agencies have jurisdiction at an incident related to their legal responsibilities and authority. Jurisdictional authority at an incident can be political or geographical (e.g., city, county, tribal, State, or Federal boundary lines) or functional (e.g., law enforcement, public health).

Jurisdictional Agency: The agency having jurisdiction and responsibility for a specific geographical area, or a mandated function.

K

Kinds of Resources: Describe what the resource is (e.g., medic, firefighter, Planning Section Chief, helicopters, ambulances, combustible gas indicators, bulldozers).

L

Landing Zone: See Helispot.

Leader: The ICS title for an individual responsible for a Task Force, Strike Team, or functional unit.

Liaison: A form of communication for establishing and maintaining mutual understanding and cooperation.

Liaison Officer (LNO): A member of the Command Staff responsible for coordinating with representatives from cooperating and assisting agencies. The Liaison Officer may have Assistants.

Logistics: Providing resources and other services to support incident management.

Logistics Section: The Section responsible for providing facilities, services, and materials for the incident.

Local Government: A county, municipality, city, town, township, local public authority, school district, special district, intrastate district, council of governments (regardless of whether the council of governments is incorporated as a nonprofit corporation under State law), regional or interstate government entity, or agency or instrumentality of a local government; an Indian tribe or authorized tribal organization, or in Alaska a Native village or Alaska Regional Native Corporation; a rural community, unincorporated town or village, or other public entity. See Section 2 (10), Homeland Security Act of 2002, Public Law 107-296, 116 Stat. 2135 (2002).

M

Major Disaster: As defined under the Robert T. Stafford Disaster Relief and Emergency Assistance Act (42 U.S.C. 5122), a major disaster is any natural catastrophe (including any hurricane, tornado, storm, high water, wind-driven water, tidal wave, tsunami, earthquake, volcanic eruption, landslide, mudslide, snowstorm, or drought), or, regardless of cause, any fire, flood, or explosion, in any part of the United States, which in the determination of the President causes damage of sufficient severity and magnitude to warrant major disaster assistance under this Act to supplement the efforts and available resources of States, tribes, local governments, and disaster relief organizations in alleviating the damage, loss, hardship, or suffering caused thereby.

Management by Objective: A management approach that involves a four-step process for achieving the incident goal. The Management by Objectives approach includes the following: establishing overarching objectives; developing and issuing assignments, plans, procedures, and protocols; establishing specific, measurable objectives for various incident management functional activities and directing efforts to fulfill them, in support of defined strategic objectives; and documenting results to measure performance and facilitate corrective action.

Managers: Individuals within ICS organizational Units that are assigned specific managerial responsibilities, e.g., Staging Area Manager or Camp Manager.

Medical Unit: Functional Unit within the Service Branch of the Logistics Section responsible for the development of the Medical Emergency Plan, and for providing emergency medical treatment of incident personnel.

Message Center: The Message Center is part of the Incident Communications Center and is collocated or placed adjacent to it. It receives, records, and routes information about resources reporting to the incident, resource status, and administrative and tactical traffic.

Mitigation: The activities designed to reduce or eliminate risks to persons or property or to lessen the actual or potential effects or consequences of an incident. Mitigation measures may be implemented prior to, during, or after an incident. Mitigation measures are often guided by lessons learned from prior incidents. Mitigation involves ongoing actions to reduce exposure to, probability of, or potential loss from hazards. Measures may include zoning and building codes, floodplain buyouts, and analysis of hazard-related data to determine where it is safe to build or locate temporary facilities. Mitigation can include efforts to educate governments, businesses, and the public on measures they can take to reduce loss and injury.

Mobilization: The process and procedures used by all organizations (Federal, State, and local) for activating, assembling, and transporting all resources that have been requested to respond to or support an incident.

Mobilization Center: An off-incident location at which emergency service personnel and equipment are temporarily located pending assignment, release, or reassignment.

Multiagency Coordination (MAC): The coordination of assisting agency resources and support to emergency operations.

Multiagency Coordination Systems (MACS): Multiagency coordination systems provide the architecture to support coordination for incident prioritization, critical resource allocation, communications systems integration, and information coordination. The components of multiagency coordination systems include facilities, equipment, emergency operations centers (EOCs), specific multiagency coordination entities, personnel, procedures, and communications. These systems assist agencies and organizations to fully integrate the subsystems of the NIMS.

Multiagency Incident: An incident where one or more agencies assist a jurisdictional agency or agencies. May be single or unified command.

Mutual Aid and Assistance Agreement: Written agreement between agencies and/or jurisdictions that they will assist one another on request, by furnishing personnel, equipment, and/or expertise in a specified manner.

N

National Incident Management System (NIMS): A system mandated by HSPD-5 that provides a consistent nationwide approach for Federal, State, local, and tribal governments; the private sector; and nongovernmental organizations to work effectively and efficiently together to prepare for, respond to, and recover from domestic incidents, regardless of cause, size, or complexity. To provide for interoperability and compatibility among Federal, State, tribal, and local capabilities, the NIMS includes a core set of concepts, principles, and terminology. HSPD-5 identifies these as the ICS; multiagency coordination systems; training; identification and management of resources (including systems for classifying types of resources); qualification and certification; and the collection, tracking, and reporting of incident information and incident resources.

O

Officer: The ICS title for the personnel responsible for the Command Staff positions of Safety, Liaison, and Public Information.

Operational Period: The period of time scheduled for execution of a given set of operation actions as specified in the Incident Action Plan. Operational periods can be of various lengths, although usually not over 24 hours.

Operations Section: The Section responsible for all tactical operations at the incident. Includes Branches, Divisions and/or Groups, Task Forces, Strike Teams, Single Resources, and Staging Areas.

Out-of-Service Resources: Resources assigned to an incident but unable to respond for mechanical, rest, or personnel reasons.

P

Planning Meeting: A meeting held as needed throughout the duration of an incident, to select specific strategies and tactics for incident control operations, and for service and support planning. On larger incidents, the Planning Meeting is a major element in the development of the Incident Action Plan.

Planning Section: Responsible for the collection, evaluation, and dissemination of information related to the incident, and for the preparation and documentation of Incident Action Plans. The Section also maintains information on the current and forecasted situation, and on the status of resources assigned to the incident. Includes the Situation, Resources, Documentation, and Demobilization Units, as well as Technical Specialists.

Preparedness: The range of deliberate, critical tasks and activities necessary to build, sustain, and improve the operational capability to prevent, protect against, respond to, and recover from domestic incidents. Preparedness is a continuous process. Preparedness involves efforts at all levels of government and between government and private-sector and nongovernmental organizations to identify threats, determine vulnerabilities, and identify required resources. Within the NIMS, preparedness is operationally focused on establishing guidelines, protocols, and standards for planning, training and exercises, personnel qualification and certification, equipment certification, and publication management.

Preparedness Organizations: The groups that provide interagency coordination for domestic incident management activities in a nonemergency context. Preparedness organizations can include all agencies with a role in incident management, for prevention, preparedness, response, or recovery activities. They represent a wide variety of committees, planning groups, and other organizations that meet and coordinate to ensure the proper level of planning, training, equipping, and other preparedness requirements within a jurisdiction or area.

Prevention: Actions to avoid an incident or to intervene to stop an incident from occurring. Prevention involves actions to protect lives and property. It involves applying intelligence and other information to a range of activities that may include such countermeasures as deterrence operations; heightened inspections; improved surveillance and security operations; investigations to determine the full nature and source of the threat; public health and agricultural surveillance and testing processes; immunizations, isolation, or quarantine; and, as appropriate, specific law enforcement operations aimed at deterring, preempting, interdicting, or disrupting illegal activity and apprehending potential perpetrators and bringing them to justice.

Procurement Unit: Functional Unit within the Finance/Administration Section responsible for financial matters involving vendor contracts.

Public Information Officer (PIO): A member of the Command Staff responsible for interfacing with the public and media or with other agencies with incident-related information requirements.

R

Recorders: Individuals within ICS organizational units who are responsible for recording information. Recorders may be found in Planning, Logistics, and Finance/Administration Units.

Reinforced Response: Those resources requested in addition to the initial response.

Reporting Locations: Location or facilities where incoming resources can check in at the incident. (See Check-In.)

Resources: Personnel and major items of equipment, supplies, and facilities available or potentially available for assignment to incident operations and for which status is maintained. Resources are described by kind and type and may be used in operational support or supervisory capacities at an incident or at an EOC.

Recovery: The development, coordination, and execution of service- and site-restoration plans; the reconstitution of government operations and services; individual, private-sector, nongovernmental, and public-assistance programs to provide housing and to promote restoration; long-term care and treatment of affected persons; additional measures for social, political, environmental, and economic restoration; evaluation of the incident to identify lessons learned; postincident reporting; and development of initiatives to mitigate the effects of future incidents.

Resource Management: Efficient incident management requires a system for identifying available resources at all jurisdictional levels to enable timely and unimpeded access to resources needed to prepare for, respond to, or recover from an incident. Resource management under the NIMS includes mutual aid agreements; the use of special Federal, State, tribal, and local teams; and resource mobilization protocols.

Resources Unit: Functional Unit within the Planning Section responsible for recording the status of resources committed to the incident. The Unit also evaluates resources currently committed to the incident, the impact that additional responding resources will have on the incident, and anticipated resource needs.

Response: Activities that address the short-term, direct effects of an incident. Response includes immediate actions to save lives, protect property, and meet basic human needs. Response also includes the execution of emergency operations plans and of mitigation activities designed to limit the loss of life, personal injury, property damage, and other unfavorable outcomes. As indicated by the situation, response activities include applying intelligence and other information to lessen the effects or consequences of an incident; increased security operations; continuing investigations into nature and source of the threat; ongoing public health and agricultural surveillance and testing processes; immunizations, isolation, or quarantine; and specific law enforcement operations aimed at preempting, interdicting, or disrupting illegal activity, and apprehending actual perpetrators and bringing them to justice.

S

Safety Officer: A member of the Command Staff responsible for monitoring and assessing safety hazards or unsafe situations, and for developing measures for ensuring personnel safety. The Safety Officer may have Assistants.

Section: The organizational level having responsibility for a major functional area of incident management, e.g., Operations, Planning, Logistics, Finance/Administration, and Intelligence (if established). The section is organizationally situated between the Branch and the Incident Command.

Segment: A geographical area in which a Task Force/Strike Team Leader or Supervisor of a single resource is assigned authority and responsibility for the coordination of resources and implementation of planned tactics. A segment may be a portion of a Division or an area inside or outside the perimeter of an incident. Segments are identified with Arabic numbers.

Service Branch: A Branch within the Logistics Section responsible for service activities at the incident. Includes the Communications, Medical, and Food Units.

Single Resource: An individual, a piece of equipment and its personnel complement, or a crew or team of individuals with an identified work Supervisor that can be used on an incident.

Situation Unit: Functional Unit within the Planning Section responsible for the collection, organization, and analysis of incident status information, and for analysis of the situation as it progresses. Reports to the Planning Section Chief.

Span of Control: The number of individuals a supervisor is responsible for, usually expressed as the ratio of supervisors to individuals. (Under the NIMS, an appropriate span of control is between 1:3 and 1:7.)

Staging Area: Location established where resources can be placed while awaiting a tactical assignment. The Operations Section manages Staging Areas.

State: When capitalized, refers to any State of the United States, the District of Columbia, the Commonwealth of Puerto Rico, the Virgin Islands, Guam, American Samoa, the Commonwealth of the Northern Mariana Islands, and any possession of the United States. See Section 2 (14), Homeland Security Act of 2002, Public Law 107-296, 116 Stat. 2135 (2002).

Strategy: The general direction selected to accomplish incident objectives set by the Incident Commander.

Strategic: Strategic elements of incident management are characterized by continuous long-term, high-level planning by organizations headed by elected or other senior officials. These elements involve the adoption of long-range goals and objectives, the setting of priorities, the establishment of budgets and other fiscal decisions, policy development, and the application of measures of performance or effectiveness.

Strike Team: A specified combination of the same kind and type of resources with common communications and a Leader.

Supervisor: The ICS title for individuals responsible for a Division or Group.

Supply Unit: Functional Unit within the Support Branch of the Logistics Section responsible for ordering equipment and supplies required for incident operations.

Support Branch: A Branch within the Logistics Section responsible for providing personnel, equipment, and supplies to support incident operations. Includes the Supply, Facilities, and Ground Support Units.

Supporting Materials: Refers to the several attachments that may be included with an Incident Action Plan, e.g., Communications Plan, Map, Safety Plan, Traffic Plan, and Medical Plan.

Support Resources: Nontactical resources under the supervision of the Logistics, Planning, or Finance/Administration Sections, or the Command Staff.

T

Tactical Direction: Direction given by the Operations Section Chief that includes the tactics required to implement the selected strategy, the selection and assignment of resources to carry out the tactics, directions for tactics implementation, and performance monitoring for each operational period.

Tactics: Deploying and directing resources on an incident to accomplish incident strategy and objectives.

Task Force: A combination of single resources assembled for a particular tactical need with common communications and a Leader.

Team: See Single Resource.

Technical Specialists: Personnel with special skills that can be used anywhere within the ICS organization.

Threat: An indication of possible violence, harm, or danger.

Time Unit: Functional Unit within the Finance/Administration Section responsible for recording time for incident personnel and hired equipment.

Type: A classification of resources in the ICS that refers to capability. Type 1 is generally considered to be more capable than Types 2, 3, or 4, respectively, because of size, power, capacity, or, in the case of Incident Management Teams, experience and qualifications.

Tools: Those instruments and capabilities that allow for the professional performance of tasks, such as information systems, agreements, doctrine, capabilities, and legislative authorities.

Tribal: Any Indian tribe, band, nation, or other organized group or community, including any Alaskan Native Village as defined in or established pursuant to the Alaskan Native Claims Settlement Act (85 Stat. 688) (43 U.S.C.A. and 1601 et seq.), that is recognized as eligible for the special programs and services provided by the United States to Indians because of their status as Indians.

U

Unified Area Command: A Unified Area Command is established when incidents under an Area Command are multijurisdictional. (See Area Command and Unified Command.)

Unified Command: An application of ICS used when there is more than one agency with incident jurisdiction or when incidents cross political jurisdictions. Agencies work together through the designated members of the Unified Command, often the senior person from agencies and/or disciplines participating in the Unified Command, to establish a common set of objectives and strategies and a single Incident Action Plan.

Unit: The organizational element having functional responsibility for a specific incident Planning, Logistics, or Finance/Administration activity.

Unity of Command: The concept by which each person within an organization reports to one and only one designated person. The purpose of unity of command is to ensure unity of effort under one responsible commander for every objective.

Unit 2: ICS Overview

Objectives

At the end of this unit, the participants should be able to:

- Identify three purposes of the Incident Command System (ICS).
- Identify requirements to use ICS.

Scope

- Unit Introduction
- Unit Objectives
- ICS Overview
  - What Is an Incident?
  - What Is ICS?
  - ICS Benefits
- History of ICS
  - Video: History of ICS
  - Activity
  - Why Use ICS?
  - Voices of Experience
- National Preparedness and ICS Requirements
- Case Study: Management Challenges
- Summary

Methodology

The instructors will introduce the unit by displaying a visual, which outlines the unit objectives. After this introduction to ICS, the instructors will lead a discussion about when participants have used ICS in the past and when they might use it in the future.

The instructors will show a video presentation that explains why ICS was initially developed. After the video, the instructors will summarize the key points of the video. To ensure comprehension, the participants will answer questions about ICS.

The instructors will introduce the group to the importance of the National Incident Management System (NIMS) and its impact on ICS.

The participants will then break into small groups to participate in a scenario-based activity in which they explore how ICS can help to address incident management challenges.

After answering any questions that the participants have, the instructors will summarize the key points from the unit and transition to Unit 3.

Time Plan

A suggested time plan for this unit is shown below. More or less time may be required, based on the experience level of the group.

Topic	Time
Unit Introduction and Unit Objectives	5 minutes
ICS Overview	15 minutes
History of ICS	10 minutes
National Preparedness and ICS Requirements	10 minutes
Case Study: Management Challenges	15 minutes
Summary	5 minutes
Total Time	**1 hour**

| Topic | Unit Introduction |

Visual 2.1

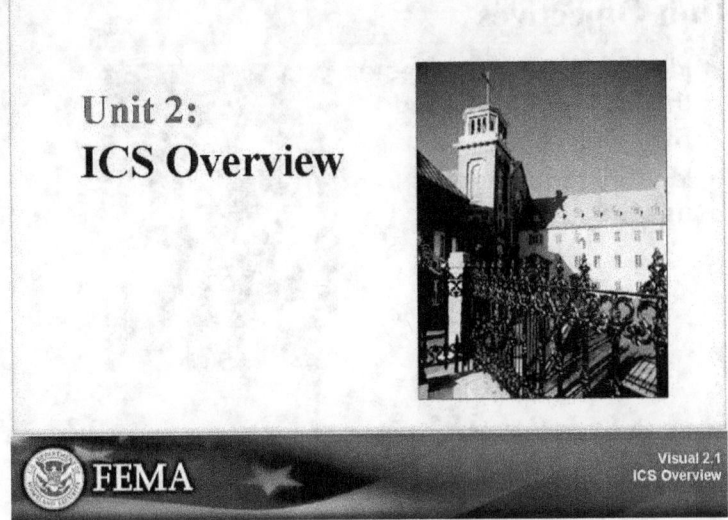

Unit 2:
ICS Overview

FEMA

Visual 2.1
ICS Overview

Visual Description: Unit Introduction

Instructor Notes

Explain that Unit 2 provides a general overview of the Incident Command System, or ICS. The next visual will outline the objectives for this unit.

Topic	Unit Objectives

Visual 2.2

Unit Objectives

- Identify three purposes of the Incident Command System (ICS).
- Identify requirements to use ICS.

FEMA

Visual 2.2
ICS Overview

Visual Description: Unit Objectives

Instructor Notes

Review the unit objectives with the group. Tell the participants that by the end of this unit, they should be able to:

- Identify three purposes of the Incident Command System (ICS).
  - Using management best practices, ICS helps to ensure:
    - The safety of responders and others.
    - The achievement of tactical objectives.
    - The efficient use of resources.

- Identify requirements to use ICS.
  - National Incident Management Systems (NIMS)
  - Superfund Amendments and Reauthorization Act (SARA) – 1986
  - Occupational Safety and Health Administration (OSHA) Rule 1910.120
  - State and Local Regulations

Topic	What Is an Incident?

Visual 2.3

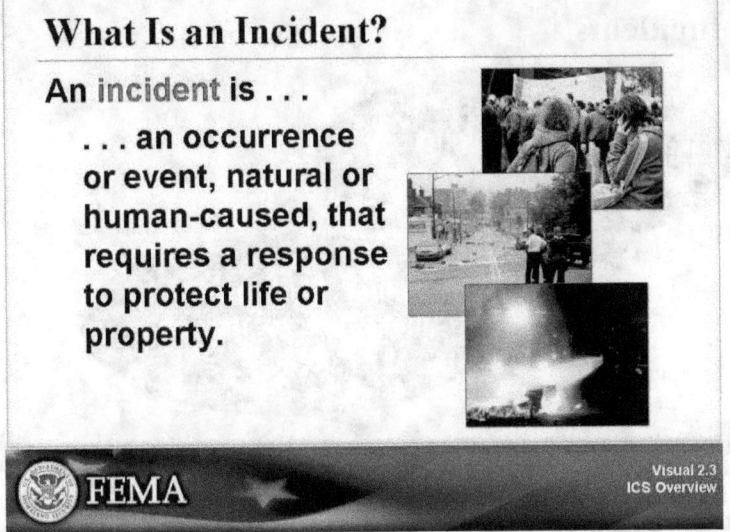

Visual Description: What Is an Incident?

Instructor Notes

Explain that an incident is an occurrence or event, natural or human-caused, that requires a response to protect life or property.

Ask the participants for examples of incidents that have occurred at higher education institutions.

Responses may include the following:

- Bomb threat/detonation (e.g., 1970 University of Wisconsin – Madison bombing)
- Hostage situation (e.g, 1992 Concordia University Massacre)
- Fire (e.g., 2007 Pepperdine University fire; 1999 Texas A&M bonfire collapse)
- Hazardous materials release (e.g., 2008 train derailment near Southern Arkansas University)
- Severe weather (e.g., 2008 Union University tornado)
- Earthquake (e.g., 1994 Cal State Northridge earthquake)
- Armed intruder on campus (e.g., 2007 Virginia Tech Massacre)

Instructor Note: Add any other local examples not mentioned by participants.

Topic	Incidents

Visual 2.4

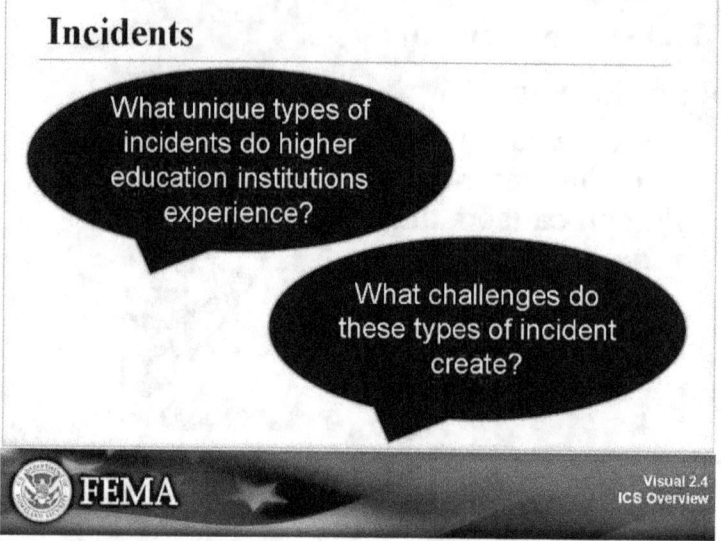

Visual Description: Discussion Questions: What unique types of incidents do higher education institutions experience? What challenges do these types of incident create?

Instructor Notes

Facilitate a discussion by asking the participants:

What unique types of incidents do higher education institutions experience?

What challenges do these types of incident create?

| Topic | Incidents |

Visual 2.5

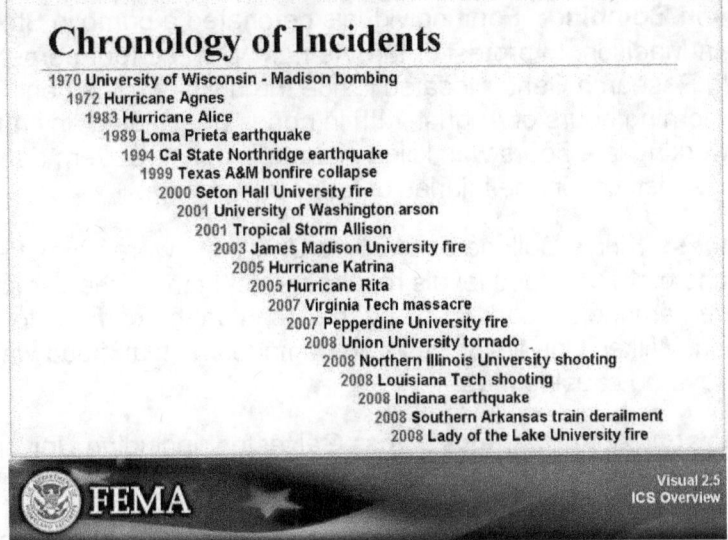

Chronology of Incidents

1970 University of Wisconsin - Madison bombing
1972 Hurricane Agnes
1983 Hurricane Alice
1989 Loma Prieta earthquake
1994 Cal State Northridge earthquake
1999 Texas A&M bonfire collapse
2000 Seton Hall University fire
2001 University of Washington arson
2001 Tropical Storm Allison
2003 James Madison University fire
2005 Hurricane Katrina
2005 Hurricane Rita
2007 Virginia Tech massacre
2007 Pepperdine University fire
2008 Union University tornado
2008 Northern Illinois University shooting
2008 Louisiana Tech shooting
2008 Indiana earthquake
2008 Southern Arkansas train derailment
2008 Lady of the Lake University fire

FEMA

Visual 2.5
ICS Overview

Visual Description: Chronology of Incidents

Instructor Notes

Briefly review the chronology of campus incidents on the visual and refer the participants to the following pages in their Student Manuals for more information about each incident.

8/24/1970 UW- Madison Bombing: Four individuals detonated a bomb in Sterling Hall at the University of Wisconsin-Madison. In protest of the Vietnam War the four perpetrators decided to destroy the Army Math Research Center located inside the building. The bomb was set to detonate in the early morning hours of August 24th in hopes of avoiding any human harm. A researcher who was working late hours was killed in the explosion. Severe damage was caused to surrounding buildings resulting in the injuries of four other people.

6/1972 Hurricane Agnes: King's College and Wilkes University were both affected by Hurricane Agnes in June of 1972. Flood levels reached waist high on the campus of King's College causing severe damage. A marker has been placed on the campus to show how high the flood levels reached. Wilkes University was also damaged by high flood waters and electrical wires were severed causing fires.

8/1983 Hurricane Alicia: Major power loss across Galveston, including University of Texas Medical Branch. Prompted new emergency power systems—generators, transfer switches, etc.

9/17/1989 Loma Prieta Earthquake: This earthquake occurred on the San Andreas Fault northeast of Santa Cruz, California. An estimated $160 million in structural damages were incurred alone with several universities being affected. Stanford University, University of California (UC) Santa Cruz University, and UC Berkeley were all affected by this quake. Unlike Stanford and Santa Cruz, UC Berkeley held classes the following day after the earthquake. This incident prompted university officials to update and change their emergency plans to be able to care, feed and shelter students and employees in the event of such a disaster occurring again. Also, building plans would be changed to deal with strong earthquakes.

1/17/1994 Cal State Northridge Earthquake: California State University, Northridge suffered severe damage from an earthquake in 1994. Several buildings such as the Fine Arts Building, the South Library, and a large parking structure were damaged beyond repair. Other buildings such as the Art Building and Main Library were damaged but were later repaired.

3/29/1998 Gustavus Adolpus Tornado: In March of 1998 an F-3 tornado that was one-mile wide struck the campus of Gustavus Adolphus in St. Peter, MN. The tornado caused $50 million dollars in damage. Fortunately no students were killed in the storm since the college was closed for spring break. The chapel on campus suffered major damage to its steeple, and many other buildings were damaged, forcing students to take classes in FEMA trailers for several weeks.

11/18/1999 Texas A&M Bonfire Collapse: A long-time tradition at Texas A&M has been the Aggie Bonfire. Students construct a large bonfire using large logs. On November 18, 1999, the 40-foot bonfire consisting of 5,000 logs collapsed during construction, resulting in 12 deaths and 27 injuries.

(Continued on next page.)

1/19/2000 Seton Hall University Fire: This university fire was a fatal fire in Boland Hall, a freshman dormitory on the Seton Hall University campus in South Orange, New Jersey. Three students died and many more were injured. Students were evacuated. The response to the incident was by the local fire department, which has indicated that there is a "difficult expectation placed on the small department to cover both the town and Seton Hall University." It was one of the deadliest college fires in recent U.S. history and has caused many officials to consider harsher penalties for pranks to fire alarms and stricter fire safety measures. This fire was caused by two students playing a prank, who faced trial and sentences.

5/21/2001 University of Washington Arson: Merrill Hall, the Center for Urban Horticulture on the campus of the University of Washington, was attacked by arsonist from the ELF (Earth Liberation Front) which is a group of "Eco Terrorists" opposed the practice of genetically modifying plants. The arson caused millions of dollars worth of damage to the facility as well as the loss of valuable research.

6/2001 Tropical Storm Allison: When Tropical Storm Allison made landfall in Texas in June of 2001 the Texas Medical Center received damage estimated at over $2 billion dollars. Important research facilities were severely damaged or completely lost. Many universities used the medical facility for research and education. The Baylor College of Medicine, Texas Woman's University Institution of Health Sciences, and the Prairie View A&M College of Nursing are just a few of many educational institutes who call the medical center home.

11/23/2003 James Madison University Fire: An office, leased from the university by a doctor, was connected to the school offices, both of which caught on fire due to a bad extension cord. There were no injuries or deaths, but much of the school's vital information and financial records were destroyed. The university's EOP was credited for the school's quick recovery.

9/16/2004 Hurricane Ivan hits University of West Florida: The University of West Florida was closed for 3 weeks after Hurricane Ivan caused damage to 95 percent of the campus buildings.

8/25-29/2005 Hurricane Katrina: This hurricane made two landfalls in both Florida and Louisiana. The City of New Orleans was tremendously damaged with breaks in levees. Universities along the entire gulf coast were affected by this particular hurricane. Tulane alone incurred a loss of $200 million in damages, which resulted in a scale back of personnel and services. Tulane's medical branch has also scaled back its clinics to simply engaging in research. An entire 4% of the university's workforce has been laid off. The University of Southern Mississippi's campus suffered an estimated $57 million in damages. The total economic impact is estimated to be $150 billion in damages across the gulf coast, making it the costliest natural disaster in US history.

9/24/2005 Hurricane Rita: The most intense tropical cyclone ever observed in the Gulf of Mexico, Rita caused $11.3 billion in damage on the U.S. gulf coast. All patients at the University of Texas Medical Branch Hospital were transferred to other area hospitals, with minor damage to the facilities. The hurricane also caused a tornado to hit the campus of Mississippi State University, resulting in damage to many campus buildings.

(Continued on next page.)

4/16/2007 Virginia Tech University Massacre: Korean student Seung-Hui Cho killed 32 students and wounded 15 others, then shot himself. He was armed with a Glock model 19 handgun and a Walther P22 handgun. The university has come under attack for not giving proper notice in a timely manner. The university has more than 25,000 students on campus spread over 2,600 acres. This incident set the stage for all campuses to review behavioral assessment procedures.

10/21/2007 Pepperdine University Fire: The blaze consumed at least 250 acres and forced the closure of the Pacific Coast Highway. Students, faculty and staff were asked to evacuate due to the fire's proximity.

2/06/2008 Union University Tornado: A tornado damaged dormitories and other buildings including most vehicles. Nearly 50 students were sent to the hospital, nine with severe injuries. This has been the second time Union University has been hit by a tornado, lastly in 2001. The damage caused by the February 5th tornado is currently estimated at $40 million. The university has a student body of about 3,300 students.

2/14/2008 Northern Illinois University Shooting: A man opened fire in lecture hall and began shooting, killing five students and wounding 16 others before killing himself. There were a total of 21 reported injured. The first campus warning went out within 20 minutes. Police reported that they responded to the scene within two minutes. The main campus has a population of 40,000 and spans 755 acres

2/08/2008 Louisiana Tech University Shooting: A female student killed herself and two others in a Baton Rouge classroom. Police immediately blocked off streets and students were ordered to stay in classrooms. Classes were cancelled for the remainder of the day. The university has an enrollment of 10,607 students.

4/18/2008 Vincennes University, Indiana Earthquake: Buildings shook for about 15 seconds as the temblor rumbled. The university immediately activated its Emergency Operations Plan. 1,489 students were evacuated from the school's residence halls into a field while building inspections occurred. They were allowed to return once the buildings were verified to be safe to re-enter.

4/18/2008 Southern Arkansas University, Train Derailment: A train hauling chlorine derailed Friday morning near Southern Arkansas University, leading authorities to evacuate the campus and nearby residents. No one was injured, and no chlorine leaked, but the threat of a chlorine leak during the cleanup prompted officials to clear the area as a precaution. Officials estimated the evacuation involved 300 to 400 people, and it was unclear when they would be able to return. Several temporary shelters were opened in town, and students were being sent to nearby churches.

5/7/2008 Lady of the Lake University, San Antonio: A four-alarm fire drew more than 30 fire trucks and 120 firefighters—more than half the city's available resources. No injuries or deaths were reported.

| Topic | What Is ICS? |

Visual 2.6

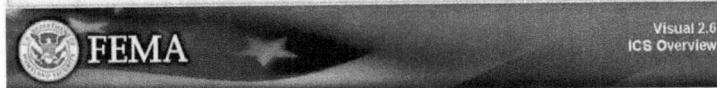

What Is ICS?

The Incident Command System:

- Is a standardized, on-scene, all-hazard incident management concept.
- Allows its users to adopt an integrated organizational structure that matches the complexities and demands of incidents.
- Permits seamless integration of responders from all jurisdictions.

FEMA

Visual 2.6
ICS Overview

Visual Description: What Is ICS?

Instructor Notes

Explain that the Incident Command System (ICS):

- Is based on proven incident management practices.

- Defines incident response organizational concepts and structures.

- Consists of procedures for managing personnel, facilities, equipment, and communications.

- Is used throughout the lifecycle on an incident (e.g., from threat to restoration of normal operations).

Topic	What Is ICS?

Visual 2.7

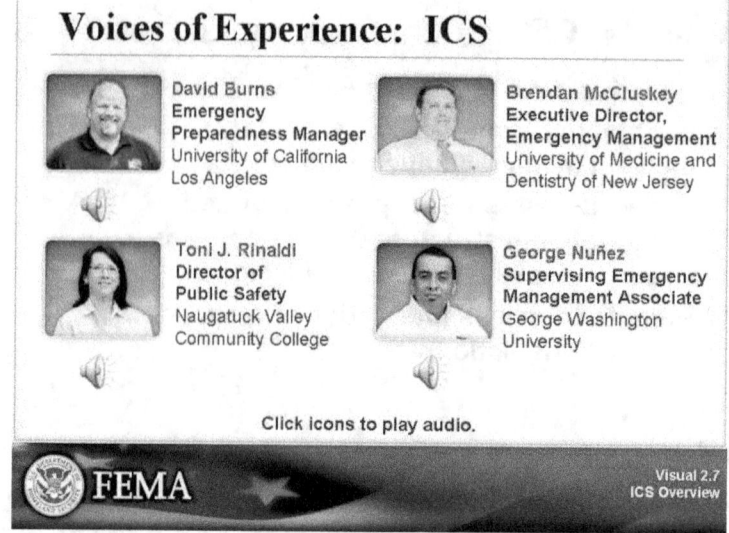

Visual Description: Voices of Experience: ICS

Instructor Notes

Tell the participants they will be hearing "voices of experience" from campus personnel about ICS.

Click on each icon to hear the "voice of experience."

Instructor note: Be sure to listen to all the audio clips before beginning the course. You may want to make note of portions that strike you as especially valuable to use as talking points while teaching.

Audio Transcripts:

David Burns
Emergency Preparedness Manager
University of California Los Angeles

ICS is a formal process for managing emergencies, tried, true, and tested for over three decades. I look at ICS as a toolbox. ICS has a set of tools and resources that almost anyone can draw from and ICS is unique and flexible enough that if I only draw off of the resources and tools that I need and I leave everything else in the box, but it's nice to know that I can draw as little or as much as I need in any given circumstance.

(Continued on next page.)

Audio Transcripts: (Continued)

Toni J. Rinaldi
Director of Public Safety
Naugatuck Valley Community College

ICS stands for the Incident Command System, and it's a standardized approach to incident management that can be used in any situation under circumstances of a large-magnitude type of incident to a very, very small-scale contained incident.

Brendan McCluskey
Executive Director, Emergency Management
University of Medicine and Dentistry of New Jersey

ICS is a tool you can use to manage the incident whether it's small or large, simple or complex, or whatever type of nature it might be, if it's a terrorist incident or a natural disaster or something else, ICS really fits all of those different things because it's so flexible.

George Nuñez
Supervising Emergency Management Associate
George Washington University

ICS is a system to allow responders to be able to organize and respond to an incident. It is specifically useful during on-scene response. It is a format, a system of tools that allow police, fire, and other personnel to respond to that incident in a systematic way to facilitate the response but also meet the needs of those impacted.

| Topic | ICS Benefits |

Visual 2.8

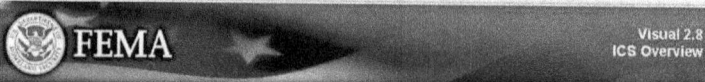

ICS Benefits

Using management best practices, ICS helps to ensure:

- The safety of responders, students, faculty, workers, and others.
- The achievement of response objectives.
- The efficient use of resources.

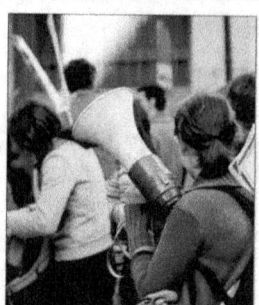

FEMA

Visual 2.8
ICS Overview

Visual Description: ICS Benefits

Instructor Notes

Emphasize that by using management best practices, ICS helps to ensure:

- The safety of responders, students, faculty, workers, and others.
- The achievement of response objectives.
- The efficient use of resources.

Topic	Video: History of ICS

Visual 2.9

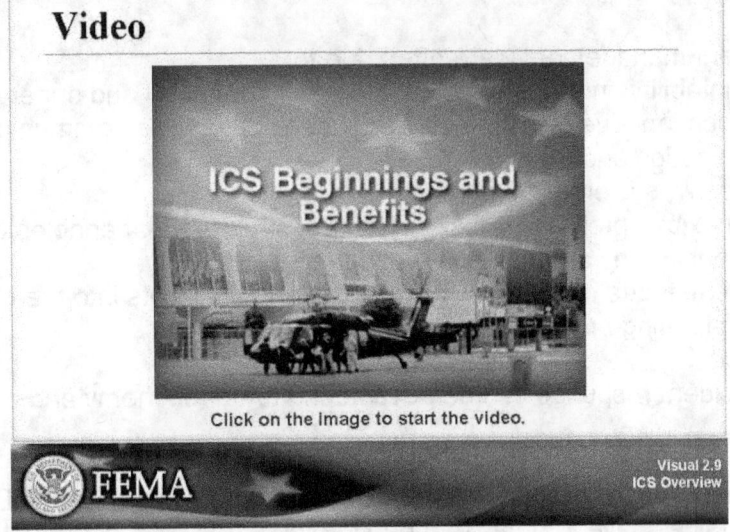

Visual Description: Video: History of ICS

Instructor Notes

Tell the participants that this video provides a brief history of the development of ICS.

Instructions for playing the video: The videos are activated by a single click on the image in Slide Show mode. If you click a second time on the video, it will stop. The videos will not work unless you are in Slide Show mode.

Video Transcript:

[Narration]
The Incident Command System (ICS) was developed in the 1970s following a series of catastrophic fires in California. Property damage ran into the millions, and many people died or were injured. The personnel assigned to determine the causes of this disaster studied the case histories and discovered that response problems could rarely be attributed to lack of resources or failure of tactics.

What were the lessons learned?
Surprisingly, studies found that response problems were far more likely to result from inadequate management than from any other single reason.

(Continued on next page.)

Video Transcript: (Continued)

Weaknesses in incident management were often due to:
- Lack of accountability, including unclear chains of command and supervision.
- Poor communication, due to both inefficient uses of available communications systems and conflicting codes and terminology.
- Lack of an orderly, systematic planning process.
- No common, flexible, predesigned management structure that enables commanders to delegate responsibilities and manage workloads efficiently.
- No predefined methods to integrate interagency requirements into the management structure and planning process effectively.

A poorly managed incident response can be devastating to our economy and our health and safety.

[Richard Lee, Assistant Director of Public Safety, University of Massachusetts Boston]
Campuses and universities have to be able to provide the same level of protection on that campus that these people enjoy when they're at home.

[Narration]
With so much at stake, we must be able to effectively manage our response efforts. The Incident Command System, or I-C-S, allows us to do so.

[Dorothy Miller, Emergency Management Coordinator, University of Texas at Dallas]
It's not just for fire even though we all know that's where it was created. It gives us a structure. It gives us a management tool.

[Paul Dean, Deputy Chief of Police/Director of Emergency Management, University of New Hampshire]
ICS is critical, it's absolutely critical for any college campus to have. Those who do not embrace it will find themselves in difficulties when an emergency happens, and in today's day and age, no one can say anymore, "I didn't know."

[end of transcript]

ICS Background

The concept of ICS was developed more than 30 years ago, in the aftermath of a devastating wildfire in California. During 13 days in 1970, 16 lives were lost, 700 structures were destroyed, and over one-half million acres burned. The overall cost and loss associated with these fires totaled $18 million per day. Although all of the responding agencies cooperated to the best of their ability, numerous problems with communication and coordination hampered their effectiveness.

As a result, the Congress mandated that the U.S. Forest Service design a system that would "make a quantum jump in the capabilities of Southern California wildland fire protection agencies to effectively coordinate interagency action and to allocate suppression resources in dynamic, multiple-fire situations."

The California Department of Forestry and Fire Protection; the Governor's Office of Emergency Services; the Los Angeles, Ventura, and Santa Barbara County Fire Departments; and the Los Angeles City Fire Department joined with the U.S. Forest Service to develop the system. This system became known as FIRESCOPE (FIrefighting RESources of California Organized for Potential Emergencies). In 1973, the first "FIRESCOPE Technical Team" was established to guide the research and development design. Two major components came out of this work, the ICS and the Multiagency Coordination System (MACS).

The FIRESCOPE ICS is primarily a command-and-control system delineating job responsibilities and organizational structure for the purpose of managing day-to-day operations for all types of emergency incidents. By the mid-seventies, the FIRESCOPE agencies had formally agreed on ICS common terminology and procedures and conducted limited field-testing of ICS. By 1980, parts of ICS had been used successfully on several major wildland and urban fire incidents. It was formally adopted by the Los Angeles Fire Department, the California Department of Forestry and Fire Protection (CDF), and the Governor's Office of Emergency Services (OES), and endorsed by the State Board of Fire Services.

Also during the 1970s, the National Wildfire Coordinating Group (NWCG) was chartered to coordinate fire management programs of the various participating Federal and State agencies.

By 1980, FIRESCOPE ICS training was under development. Recognizing that in addition to the local users for which it was designed, the FIRESCOPE training could satisfy the needs of other State and Federal agencies, the NWCG conducted an analysis of FIRESCOPE ICS for possible national application.

By 1981, ICS was widely used throughout Southern California by the major fire agencies. In addition, the use of ICS in response to nonfire incidents was increasing. Although FIRESCOPE ICS was originally developed to assist in the response to wildland fires, it was quickly recognized as a system that could help public safety responders provide effective and coordinated incident management for a wide range of situations, including floods, hazardous materials accidents, earthquakes, and aircraft crashes. It was flexible enough to manage catastrophic incidents involving thousands of emergency response and management personnel.

In 1982, all FIRESCOPE ICS documentation was revised and adopted as the National Interagency Incident Management System (NIIMS). In the years since FIRESCOPE and the NIIMS were blended, the FIRESCOPE agencies and the NWCG have worked together to update and maintain the Incident Command System Operational System Description (ICS 120-1). This document would later serve as the basis for the National Incident Management System (NIMS) ICS.

By introducing relatively minor terminology, organizational, and procedural modifications to FIRESCOPE ICS, the NIIMS ICS became adaptable to an all-hazards environment. While tactically each type of incident may be handled somewhat differently, the overall incident management approach still utilizes the major functions of the Incident Command System. The FIRESCOPE board of directors and the NWCG recommended national application of ICS.

ICS Variations

In the early 1970s, the Phoenix Fire Department developed the Fire Ground Command System (FGC). The concepts of FGC were similar to FIRESCOPE ICS but there were differences in terminology and in organizational structure. The FGC system was developed for structural firefighting and was designed for operations of 25 or fewer companies.

There were several efforts to "blend" the various incident command systems. One early effort was in 1987 when the National Fire Protection Association (NFPA) undertook the development of NFPA 1561, then called Standard on Fire Department Incident Management System. The NFPA committee quickly recognized that the majority of the incident command systems in existence at the time were similar.

The differences among the systems were mostly due to variations in terminology for similar components. That NFPA standard, later revised to its present title: Standard on Emergency Services Incident Management, provides for organizations to adopt or modify existing systems to suit local requirements or preferences as long as they meet specific performance measurements. Recognizing the continuing challenges occurring in the fire service in applying a common approach to incident command, the National Fire Service Incident Management System (IMS) Consortium was created in 1990. Its purpose was to evaluate an approach to developing a single command system. The consortium consisted of many individual fire service leaders, representatives of most major fire service organizations, and representatives of Federal, State, and local agencies, including FIRESCOPE and the Phoenix Fire Department. One of the significant outcomes of the consortium's work was an agreement on the need to develop operational protocols within ICS, so that fire and rescue personnel would be able to apply the ICS as one common system.

In 1993, the IMS consortium completed its first document: Model Procedures Guide for Structural Firefighting. As a result, FIRESCOPE incorporated the model procedures, thereby enhancing its organizational structure with operational protocols. These changes enabled the Nation's fire and rescue personnel to apply the ICS effectively regardless of what region of the country they were assigned to work. The National Fire Academy (NFA), having already adopted the FIRESCOPE ICS in 1980, incorporated this material into its training curriculum as well.

Source: National Integration Center

| Topic | Activity |

Visual 2.10

Activity: ICS & Planned Events

Instructions: Working as a team . . .

- Briefly describe one example where ICS could be used to manage planned events (e.g., sporting events) on your campus.

- Identify the benefits of using ICS for the selected event.

- Select a spokesperson and be prepared to present your example.

FEMA

Visual 2.10
ICS Overview

Visual Description: Activity: ICS & Planned Events

Instructor Notes

Purpose: The purpose of this activity is to illustrate how ICS can be used to address incident management issues, using planned events as an example.

Instructions: Follow the steps below to conduct this activity:

1. Assign the participants to work as a team to develop a brief description of one example where ICS could be used to manage planned events on campus. Participants should also identify the benefits of using ICS for the selected event.
2. Tell the groups to write their examples on chart paper.
3. Ask the participants in each group to select a spokesperson to present the group's response.
4. Tell the groups that they will have 5 minutes to complete this activity.

Debrief:

1. Monitor the time. When 5 minutes have passed, ask the spokesperson from each group to briefly present their response.
2. Point out the importance of practicing ICS in planned events such as athletic events, parades, commencements, and other large gatherings on campus.
3. If not mentioned by the groups, emphasize the importance of including outside response agencies in the ICS organization for planned events.

| Topic | Why Use ICS? |

Visual 2.11

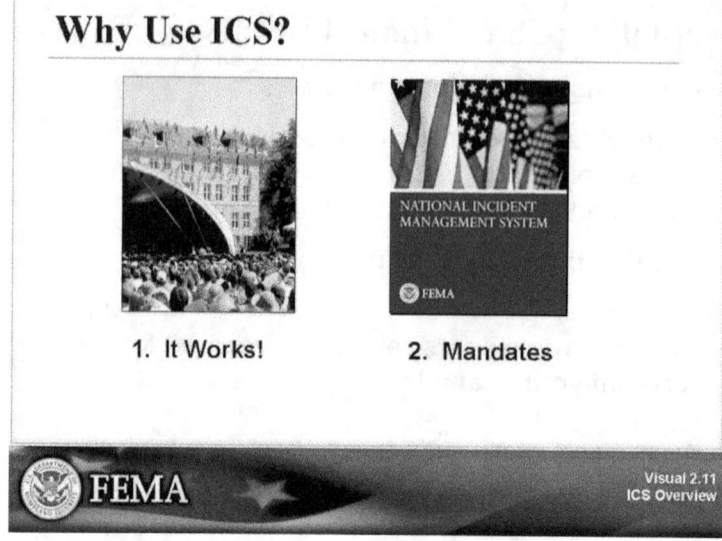

Visual Description: Why Use ICS?

Instructor Notes

Present the following points about the value of using ICS:

- It works! Tell the participants that in the next part of this unit, they'll hear about several ICS success stories.

- The use of ICS is mandated by the National Incident Management System (NIMS). NIMS provides a systematic, proactive approach guiding departments and agencies at all levels of government, the private sector, and nongovernmental organizations to work seamlessly to prepare for, prevent, respond to, recover from, and mitigate the effects of incidents, regardless of cause, size, location, or complexity, in order to reduce the loss of life and property, and harm to the environment.

Topic	Voices of Experience

Visual 2.12

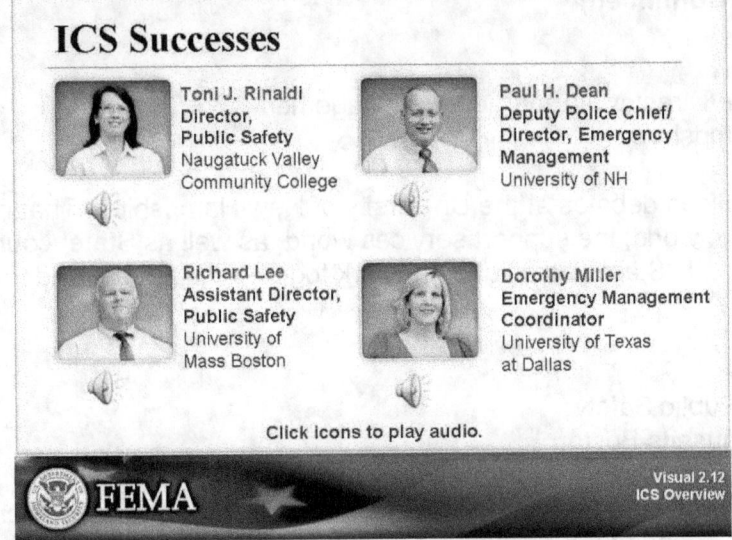

Visual Description: ICS Successes

Instructor Notes

Tell the participants they will be hearing "voices of experience" from campus personnel about the successful use of ICS on their campuses.

Click on each image to hear the "voice of experience."

Audio Transcripts:

Toni J. Rinaldi
Director of Public Safety
Naugatuck Valley Community College

We had a very suspicious package that was possibly an explosive device that was placed near a trash can on the second floor of a two-story parking garage facility that sits under a fourth floor academic building. It was reported to public safety and immediately all the players went into action. The initial responder who became the original incident commander took control of the situation and started delegating functional roles that were needed. . . Fortunately, the whole incident was brought to a successful conclusion after about an hour and a half or two hours.

Audio Transcripts: (Continued)

Paul H. Dean
Deputy Chief of Police/Director of Emergency Management
University of New Hampshire

We hosted the Republican debates at the University of New Hampshire. That brought in a variety of the academic world, the support services world, as well as State, county, and Federal assets into the system. ICS allowed all of us to work together as a team and for a successful event.

Richard Lee
Assistant Director of Public Safety
University of Massachusetts Boston

We had what was called a straight-lined thunderstorm come through with a microburst in it which tore the roof off of one of our buildings, and we used our incident command system. We had appointed an incident commander who happened to be our facilities director who then started giving orders about how to make sure power was shut down, what needed to be covered up, and all the other incidents that needed to be in there such as monitoring alarms and everything else, and it eventually settled back down from then and we worked it into then where our public safety director took over and was charged with working the perimeters and everything else until the incident was resolved.

Dorothy Miller
Emergency Management Coordinator
University of Texas at Dallas

During a hazmat incident at one of our buildings that houses chemistry labs, when I got to the scene there was already an incident command post set up, the fire chief was in charge, and there of course was the hazmat teams called out, environmental heath and safety, the police chief. I talked to the police and fire chiefs because I know who they are. I had ahead of time made that relationship establishment. That's incredibly important that when you train, you can't just have your classes in a vacuum. You have to include all the responders in your community also and possibly other campuses because everyone has a different perspective but also you may need them in the future so you need to know who they are ahead of time.

Topic	National Preparedness and ICS Requirements

Visual 2.13

National Incident Management System (NIMS)

What ? . . . NIMS provides a consistent nationwide template . . .

Who? . . . to enable Federal, State, tribal, and local governments, the private sector, and nongovernmental organizations to work together . . .

How? . . . to prepare for, prevent, respond to, recover from, and mitigate the effects of incidents regardless of cause, size, location, or complexity . . .

Why? . . . in order to reduce the loss of life and property, and harm to the environment.

FEMA

Visual 2.13
ICS Overview

Visual Description: National Incident Management System (NIMS)

Instructor Notes

Explain to the participants that **the National Incident Management System (NIMS) provides a consistent framework for incident management at all jurisdictional levels regardless of the cause, size, or complexity of the incident.** NIMS is not an operational incident management or resource allocation plan.

Visual 2.14

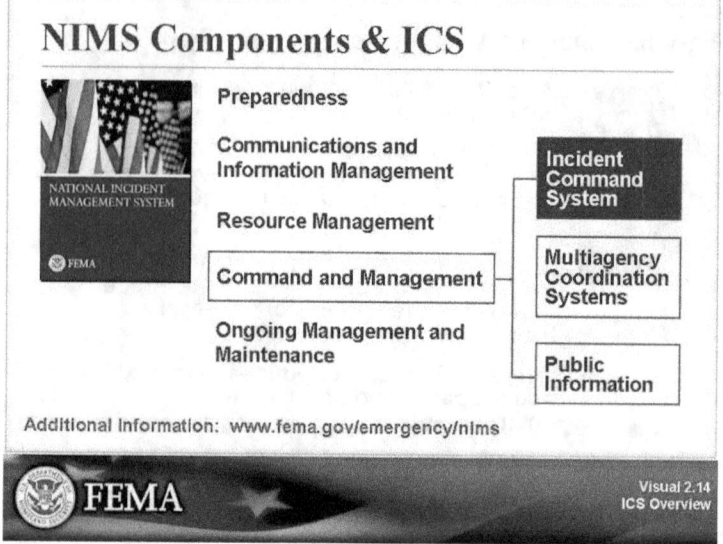

Visual Description: NIMS Components & ICS

Instructor Notes

Tell the participants that NIMS represents a core set of doctrine, concepts, principles, terminology, and organizational processes that enables effective, efficient, and collaborative incident management.

- **Preparedness:** Effective emergency management and incident response activities begin with a host of preparedness activities conducted on an ongoing basis, in advance of any potential incident. Preparedness involves an integrated combination of planning, procedures and protocols, training and exercises, personnel qualifications and certification, and equipment certification.

- **Communications and Information Management:** Emergency management and incident response activities rely upon communications and information systems that provide a common operating picture to all command and coordination sites. NIMS describes the requirements necessary for a standardized framework for communications and emphasizes the need for a common operating picture. NIMS is based upon the concepts of interoperability, reliability, scalability, portability, and the resiliency and redundancy of communications and information systems.

- **Resource Management:** Resources (such as personnel, equipment, and/or supplies) are needed to support critical incident objectives. The flow of resources must be fluid and adaptable to the requirements of the incident. NIMS defines standardized mechanisms and establishes the resource management process to: identify requirements, order and acquire, mobilize, track and report, recover and demobilize, reimburse, and inventory resources.

(Continued on next page.)

- **Command and Management:** The Command and Management component within NIMS is designed to enable effective and efficient incident management and coordination by providing flexible, standardized incident management structures. The structures are based on three key organizational constructs: **the Incident Command System, Multiagency Coordination Systems, and Public Information.**

- **Ongoing Management and Maintenance:** Within the auspices of Ongoing Management and Maintenance, there are two components: the National Integration Center (NIC) and Supporting Technologies.

Topic | **National Preparedness and ICS Requirements**

Visual 2.15

ICS Mandates

NIMS requires all levels of government to:

- Prepare for and use ICS for all domestic responses.
- Adopt ICS as a condition of receiving Federal preparedness funding including U.S. Department of Education Emergency Management for Higher Education (EMHE) grants.

FEMA

Visual 2.15
ICS Overview

Visual Description: ICS Mandates

Instructor Notes

Adopting ICS and NIMS is a condition of receiving Federal preparedness funding and certain grants.

ICS will help you implement Federal, State, and local mandates, such as Clery Act regulations for campus security and crime statistics. The Clery Act, named for a college freshman who was raped and murdered in a campus residence hall, requires colleges and universities to maintain and disclose information about crime on and around their campuses.

According to the National Integration Center, "institutionalizing the use of ICS" means that government officials, incident managers, and emergency response organizations at all jurisdictional levels must adopt the Incident Command System. Actions to institutionalize the use of ICS take place at two levels:

Policy Level: At the policy level, institutionalizing the ICS means government officials (i.e., Governors, mayors, county and city managers, tribal leaders, and others) must:

- Adopt the ICS through executive order, proclamation, or legislation as the jurisdiction's official incident response system; and
- Direct that incident managers and response organizations in their jurisdictions train, exercise, and use the ICS in their response operations.

Organizational Level: At the organizational/operational level, evidence that incident managers and emergency response organizations are institutionalizing the ICS would include the following:

- ICS is being integrated into functional and system-wide emergency operations policies, plans, and procedures.
- ICS training is planned or underway for responders, supervisors, and command-level officers.
- Responders at all levels are participating in and/or coordinating ICS-oriented exercises that involve responders from multiple disciplines and jurisdictions.

Visual 2.16

Other ICS Mandates

- Hazardous Materials Incidents
  - Superfund Amendments and Reauthorization Act (SARA) – 1986
  - Occupational Safety and Health Administration (OSHA) Rule 1910.120
- State and Local Regulations

FEMA

Visual 2.16
ICS Overview

Visual Description: Other ICS Mandates

Instructor Notes

Explain that in addition to the NIMS mandate, the following laws require the use of ICS:

- The Superfund Amendments and Reauthorization Act (SARA) of 1986 established Federal regulations for handling hazardous materials. SARA directed the Occupational Safety and Health Administration (OSHA) to establish rules for operations at hazardous materials incidents.

- OSHA rule 1910.120, effective March 6, 1990, requires all organizations that handle hazardous materials to use ICS. The regulation states: "The Incident Command System shall be established by those employers for the incidents that will be under their control and shall interface with other organizations or agencies who may respond to such an incident."

Note that the Environmental Protection Agency (EPA) requires States to use ICS at hazardous materials incidents.

IMPORTANT INSTRUCTOR NOTE: Add any State and local regulations governing the use of ICS.

Topic	Case Study: Management Challenges

Visual 2.17

Case Study: Management Challenges

Instructions:

1. Working as a team, review the case study presented in your Student Manuals.
2. Identify the top three challenges in managing this incident. Write these challenges on chart paper.
3. Using what you have learned so far, describe how ICS could be used to address these challenges.
4. Select a spokesperson. Be prepared to present in 5 minutes.

FEMA

Visual 2.17
ICS Overview

Visual Description: Case Study: Management Challenges

Instructor Notes

Purpose: The purpose of this activity is to illustrate how ICS can be used to address incident management issues.

Instructions: Follow the steps below to conduct this activity:

1. Assign the participants to groups of five or six.
2. Tell the participants to work as a team to review the scenario presented on the next page in their Student Manuals.
3. Explain that each group should identify the top three challenges for officials to manage this incident. Each group should write the challenges on chart paper. The groups should also discuss how ICS could be used to address these challenges.
4. Ask the participants in each group to select a spokesperson.
5. Inform the group that they will have 5 minutes to complete this activity.

| Topic | Case Study: Management Challenges |

Instructions: The purpose of this scenario is to demonstrate the benefits of ICS. Review the following scenario and then lead the participants in a discussion using the questions below. Use the discussion to point out the benefits of ICS. Indicate what might happen if ICS is not used to manage this situation.

Scenario: During freshman move-in, a dangerous worm has spread rapidly through the university computer network. The worm, which is consuming massive amounts of bandwidth, also includes a "payload" code designed to delete files on affected computers. The effects have essentially crippled the university computer network, including systems for course registration and emergency notification. The network is also used when students swipe their identification cards to enter residence halls and fitness facilities, and to pay for meals at campus dining halls. It remains unclear whether the incident poses a threat to sensitive information, such as student and employee Social Security numbers.

Discussion Questions:

What are the priorities?

What are the incident management challenges? (Think about how ICS may address these challenges!)

Who needs to be involved?

Instructor Note: There is no one correct answer, but if not mentioned by participants, note that using management best practices, ICS helps to ensure:
- The safety of responders and others.
- The achievement of tactical objectives.
- The efficient use of resources.

| Topic | Summary |

Visual 2.18

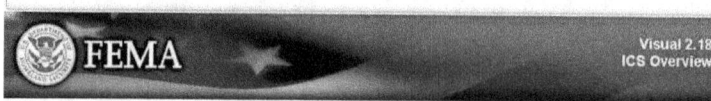

Summary

ICS . . .

- Is a standardized management tool for meeting the demands of small or large emergency and nonemergency situations.
- Represents best practices, and has become the standard for emergency management across the country.
- May be used for planned events, natural disasters, and acts of terrorism.
- Is a key feature of NIMS.

FEMA

Visual 2.18
ICS Overview

Visual Description: Summary

Instructor Notes

Summarize this unit by reminding the group that ICS:

- Is a standardized management tool for meeting the demands of small or large emergency and nonemergency situations.
- Represents best practices, and has become the standard for emergency management across the country.
- May be used for planned events, natural disasters, and acts of terrorism.
- Is a key feature of NIMS.

Ask if anyone has any questions about anything covered in this unit.

Transition to the next unit by explaining that it will cover the basic features of ICS.

Unit 3: ICS Features and Principles

Objectives

At the end of this unit, the participants should be able to describe the basic features and principles of the Incident Command System (ICS).

Scope

- Unit Introduction
- Unit Objective
- ICS Features
  - Video: ICS Features
- Standardization
  - Common Terminology – No Codes
  - Use of Plain English
- Command
  - Command: Definition
  - Transfer of Command
  - Chain of Command
  - Unity of Command
  - Incident Management Roles
  - Activity: Command
- Planning/Organizational Structure
  - Management by Objectives
  - ICS Organization
  - Modular Organization
  - Incident Action Planning (IAP)
    - Activity: IAP
  - Manageable Span of Control
    - Activity: Span of Control
- Facilities and Resources
  - Video: Incident Facilities Virtual Tour
  - Incident Facility Map Symbols
  - Resources: Definition
  - Resource Management
  - Activity: Staging Area
- Communications/Information Management
  - Integrated Communications
  - Information & Intelligence Management
  - Case Study: Incident Management
- Professionalism
  - Accountability
  - Dispatch/Deployment
  - Activity: Deployment
- Summary

Methodology

The instructors will begin by explaining that this unit provides an overview of the basic features and principles of the Incident Command System, or ICS. Instructors will display a visual that outlines the unit objectives.

After reviewing the unit objectives, the instructors will provide information on ICS features and principles, first by showing a video. Next, they will explain the importance of standardization by using common terminology and plain English during an incident response.

Next, the instructors will introduce establishment and transfer of command. They will define command and then describe the process for transferring command, or moving responsibility for incident command from one Incident Commander to another. The instructors will provide examples of situations where a transfer of command would be needed. They will ask participants to identify topics to include in a transfer of command briefing. The instructors will cover the concepts of chain of command and unity of command. The instructors will clarify the differences between the role of the Incident Commander and the role of the Executive Policy Group during an incident. The group will consider a scenario to segue into discussion of incident objectives, and the priorities followed in addressing objectives in campus incidents.

Next, the instructors will explain the differences between ICS organizational structure and day-to-day administrative organizational structure. The instructors will cover how objectives are established to manage the incident. They will describe the ICS flexible modular organization, including the fact that only functions or positions that are necessary will be filled.

The next ICS feature covered is the development of an Incident Action Plan, or IAP. The instructors will identify the four elements that every IAP must contain. The participants will then work in teams to identify four items to include in an IAP for the incident used in Unit 2.

The instructors will explain the importance of maintaining a manageable span of control: Per ICS guidelines, a supervisor optimally should not have more than 5 subordinates. The instructor will ask the participants what types of campus incident situations warrant a low span-of-control ratio. Students will consider a campus incident scenario, and determine whether the span of control is sufficient.

Next the group will view a video that presents a "virtual tour" of standard ICS facilities. The instructors will then briefly review predesignated incident facilities. The next ICS feature covered is resource management. Resources include personnel as well as equipment.

The instructors will then explain the importance of developing an integrated voice and data communications system, and ensuring that communications systems among various responders are interoperable. The instructors will lead a discussion of the importance of information and intelligence management. They will use an activity to ask the group for examples of information and intelligence that could be used to manage an incident.

The instructors will then explain the importance of professionalism, which includes applying principles of accountability and carrying out responsibilities involved in dispatch and deployment. The group will discuss complications that arise from self-deployment, and consider pros and cons of self-deployment in a campus scenario.

At the end of the unit, the participants will answer questions about the ICS features covered. The instructors will then summarize the key ICS features and principles, and transition to Unit 4.

Time Plan

A suggested time plan for this unit is shown below. More or less time may be required, based on the experience level of the group.

Topic	Time
Unit Introduction and Unit Objectives	5 minutes
ICS Features	10 minutes
Standardization	5 minutes
Command	12 minutes
Activity: Command	4 minutes
Planning/Organizational Structure	8 minutes
Activity: Incident Action Plan	10 minutes
Activity: Span of Control	3 minutes
Facilities and Resources	10 minutes
Activity: Staging Area	5 minutes
Communications/Information Management	10 minutes
Case Study: Incident Management	5 minutes
Professionalism	10 minutes
Activity: Deployment	3 minutes
Summary	5 minutes
Total Time	**1 hour 45 minutes**

This page intentionally left blank.

| Topic | Unit Introduction |

Visual 3.1

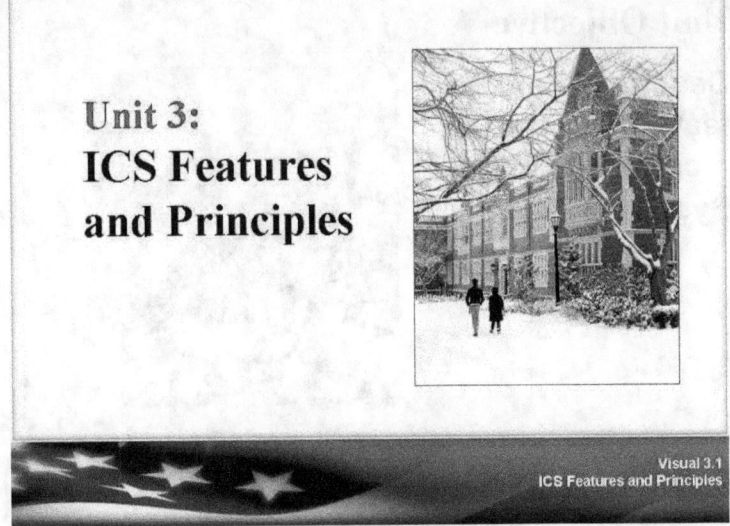

Visual Description: Unit Introduction

Instructor Notes

Tell the participants that this unit will provide an overview of the basic features and principles of the Incident Command System:

- ICS management principles
- ICS core system features

Topic   Unit Objective

Visual 3.2

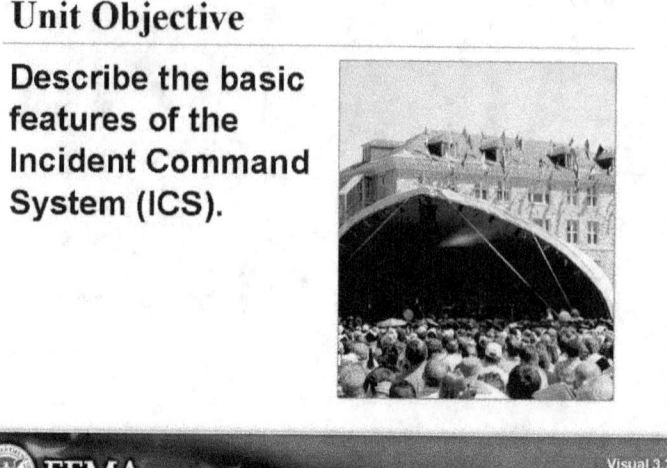

Visual Description: Unit Objective

Instructor Notes

Tell the group that by the end of this unit they should be able to describe the basic features of the Incident Command System (ICS).

Visual 3.3

ICS Features: Overview

- Standardization
  - Common terminology
- Command
  - Establishment and transfer of command
  - Chain of command and unity of command
- Planning/Organizational Structure
  - Management by objectives
  - Incident Action Plan (IAP)
  - Modular organization
  - Manageable span of control
- Facilities and Resources
  - Comprehensive resource management
  - Incident locations and facilities
- Communications/Information Management
  - Integrated communications
  - Information and intelligence management
- Professionalism
  - Accountability
  - Dispatch/Deployment

FEMA

Visual 3.3
ICS Features and Principles

Visual Description: ICS Features: Overview

Instructor Notes

Review the features presented on the visual. Refer the participants to the next two pages in their Student Manuals, which provide more detail about each feature.

Topic   **ICS Features**

The essential ICS features are listed below:

Standardization:

- **Common Terminology:** Using common terminology helps to define organizational functions, incident facilities, resource descriptions, and position titles.

Command:

- **Establishment and Transfer of Command:** The command function must be clearly established from the beginning of an incident. When command is transferred, the process must include a briefing that captures all essential information for continuing safe and effective operations.

- **Chain of Command and Unity of Command:** Chain of command refers to the orderly line of authority within the ranks of the incident management organization. Unity of command means that every individual has a designated supervisor to whom he or she reports at the scene of the incident. These principles clarify reporting relationships and eliminate the confusion caused by multiple, conflicting directives. Incident managers at all levels must be able to control the actions of all personnel under their supervision.

Planning/Organizational Structure:

- **Management by Objectives:** Includes establishing overarching objectives; developing and issuing assignments, plans, procedures, and protocols; establishing specific, measurable objectives for various incident management functional activities; and directing efforts to attain the established objectives.

- **Modular Organization:** The Incident Command organizational structure develops in a top-down, modular fashion that is based on the size and complexity of the incident, as well as the specifics of the hazard environment created by the incident.

- **Incident Action Planning:** Incident Action Plans (IAPs) provide a coherent means of communicating the overall incident objectives in the contexts of both operational and support activities.

- **Manageable Span of Control:** Span of control is key to effective and efficient incident management. Within ICS, the span of control of any individual with incident management supervisory responsibility should range from three to seven subordinates.

Facilities and Resources:

- **Incident Locations and Facilities:** Various types of operational locations and support facilities are established in the vicinity of an incident to accomplish a variety of purposes. Typical predesignated facilities include Incident Command Posts, Bases, Camps, Staging Areas, Mass Casualty Triage Areas, and others as required.

- **Comprehensive Resource Management:** Resource management includes processes for categorizing, ordering, dispatching, tracking, and recovering resources. It also includes processes for reimbursement for resources, as appropriate. Resources are defined as personnel, teams, equipment, supplies, and facilities available or potentially available for assignment or allocation in support of incident management and emergency response activities.

Communications/Information Management:

- **Integrated Communications:** Incident communications are facilitated through the development and use of a common communications plan and interoperable communications processes and architectures.

- **Information and Intelligence Management:** The incident management organization must establish a process for gathering, sharing, and managing incident-related information and intelligence.

Professionalism:

- **Accountability:** Effective accountability at all jurisdictional levels and within individual functional areas during incident operations is essential. To that end, the following principles must be adhered to:
  - **Check-In:** All responders, regardless of agency affiliation, must report in to receive an assignment in accordance with the procedures established by the Incident Commander.
  - **Incident Action Plan:** Response operations must be directed and coordinated as outlined in the IAP.
  - **Unity of Command:** Each individual involved in incident operations will be assigned to only one supervisor.
  - **Span of Control:** Supervisors must be able to adequately supervise and control their subordinates, as well as communicate with and manage all resources under their supervision.
  - **Resource Tracking:** Supervisors must record and report resource status changes as they occur. (This topic is covered in a later unit.)

- **Dispatch/Deployment:** Personnel and equipment should respond only when requested or when dispatched by an appropriate authority.

Topic   Video: ICS Features

Visual 3.4

Visual Description: Video: ICS Features

Instructor Notes

Tell the participants that the following video will introduce this lesson on ICS features and principles.

Explain that the lesson covers each of these ICS features in detail.

Video Transcript:

[Narrator]
As you learned in the previous lesson, ICS is based on proven management principles, which contribute to the strength and efficiency of the overall system.

ICS incorporates a wide range of management features, beginning with the use of common terminology and clear text.

[David Burns, Emergency Preparedness Manager, University of California Los Angeles]
Communication is probably one of the most essential elements of ICS. It's important that we know how to communicate.

[Narrator]
ICS uses a flexible, modular organizational structure.

(Continued on next page.)

Video Transcript: (Continued)

[Brendan McCluskey, Executive Director of Emergency Management, University of Medicine and Dentistry of New Jersey]
You can use it to manage the incident whether it's small or large, simple or complex or whatever type of nature. ICS really fits all of those different things because it's so flexible.

[Narrator]
ICS emphasizes effective planning, including management by objectives and reliance on an Incident Action Plan.

[George Nuñez, Supervising Emergency Management Associate, George Washington University]
One benefit of ICS is organization. It allows responders to come together regardless of their role or responsibilities and be able to organize and respond to the incident.

[Narrator]
The ICS features related to command structure include chain of command and unity of command.

[Toni Rinaldi, Director of Public Safety, Naugatuck Valley Community College]
Internally it defines everybody's role in incident management. It defines a standard set of rules that everyone is going to follow regardless of who is working on a given day, regardless of who happens to be in charge administratively that day and regardless of who's on your campus.

[Narrator]
ICS helps ensure full utilization of all incident resources by:
- Maintaining a manageable span of control,
- Establishing predesignated incident locations and facilities,
- Implementing resource management practices.,
- And ensuring integrated communications.

ICS supports responders and decisionmakers through effective information and intelligence management.

[James Hamrick, Assistant Chief of Police, University of Maryland]
ICS can help manage the large amount of information that is inherent in a large event, whether that's a critical incident or a large planned event.

[Narrator]
ICS counts on each of us taking personal accountability for our own actions.

[David Burns]
Accountability is basically a process where individuals know their responsibilities, they know their role, they know what process they contribute to.

(Continued on next page.)

| Topic | Video: ICS Features |

Video Transcript: (Continued)

[Narrator]
The mobilization process helps ensure that incident objectives can be achieved while responders and students remain safe.

[Richard Lee]
ICS gives us a common language, a common background, and a common way of doing things so that we're all working on the best, on the same page, and can best provide for the safety and security of our campuses.

[Narrator]
This lesson presents the ICS features that promote effective, team-based incident response.

[end of transcript]

| Topic | Standardization |

Visual 3.5

Common Terminology – No Codes!

Using common terminology
helps to define:

- Organizational functions.
- Incident facilities.
- Resource descriptions.
- Position titles.

Common terminology allows campus
personnel to integrate seamlessly
with community responders.

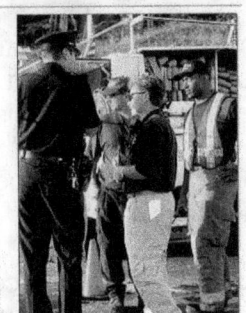

FEMA

Visual 3.5
ICS Features and Principles

Visual Description: Common Terminology – No Codes!

Instructor Notes

The ability to communicate within the ICS is absolutely critical. An essential method for ensuring the ability to communicate is by using common terminology and clear text.

A critical part of an effective multiagency incident management system is for all communications to be in plain English. That is, use clear text. Do not use radio codes, departmental codes, or jargon.

Topic   **Standardization**

ICS establishes common terminology allowing diverse incident management and support entities to work together. Common terminology helps to define:

- **Organizational Functions.** Major functions and functional units with domestic incident management responsibilities are named and defined. Terminology for the organizational elements involved is standard and consistent.

- **Incident Facilities.** Common terminology is used to designate the facilities in the vicinity of the incident area that will be used in the course of incident management activities.

- **Resource Descriptions.** Major resources—including personnel, facilities, and major equipment and supply items—used to support incident management activities are given common names and are "typed" with respect to their capabilities, to help avoid confusion and to enhance interoperability.

- **Position Titles.** At each level within the ICS organization, individuals with primary responsibility have distinct titles. Titles provide a common standard for all users, and also make it easier to fill ICS positions with qualified personnel. ICS titles often do NOT correspond to the titles used on a daily basis.

| Topic | Standardization |

Visual 3.6

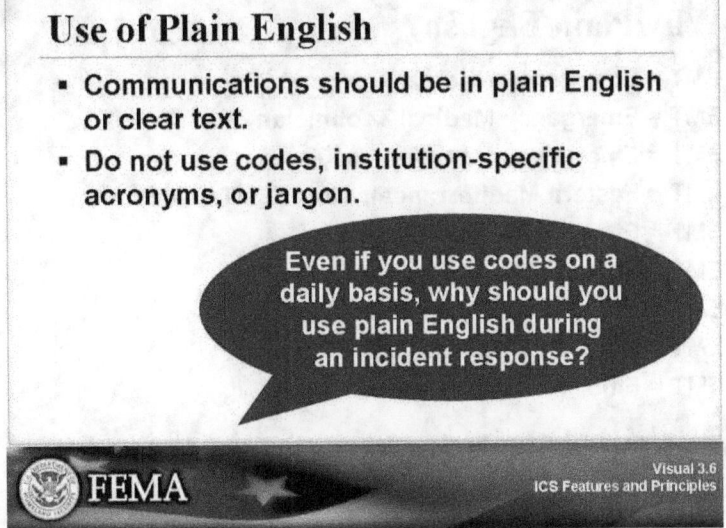

Visual Description: Use of Plain English

Instructor Notes

Ask the participants the following question:

Even if you use codes on a daily basis, why should you use plain English during an incident response?

Allow the participants time to respond.

If not mentioned by the group, tell the participants that it is important to use plain English during an incident response because often there is more than one organization involved in an incident. Ambiguous codes and acronyms have proven to be major obstacles in communications. Often organizations have a variety of codes and acronyms that they use routinely during normal operations. When these codes and acronyms are used on an incident, confusion is often the result. The National Incident Management Systems (NIMS) requires that all responders use "plain English," referred to as "clear text," and within the United States, English is the standard language.

Topic	Standardization

Visual 3.7

Why Plain English?

EMT = Emergency Medical Treatment
EMT = Emergency Medical Technician
EMT = Emergency Management Team
EMT = Eastern Mediterranean Time (GMT+0200)
EMT = Effective Methods Team
EMT = Effects Management Tool
EMT = El Monte, CA (airport code)
EMT = Electron Microscope Tomography
EMT = Email Money Transfer

FEMA

Visual 3.7
ICS Features and Principles

Visual Description: Why Plain English?

Instructor Notes

Refer the participants to the following examples of different meanings of a common acronym.

EMT = Emergency Medical Treatment
EMT = Emergency Medical Technician
EMT = Emergency Management Team
EMT = Eastern Mediterranean Time (GMT+0200)
EMT = Effective Methods Team
EMT = Effects Management Tool
EMT = El Monte, CA (airport code)
EMT = Electron Microscope Tomography
EMT = Email Money Transfer

Ask the participants for examples of other codes or jargon that could be misunderstood by responders from different agencies.

Topic	Command

Visual 3.8

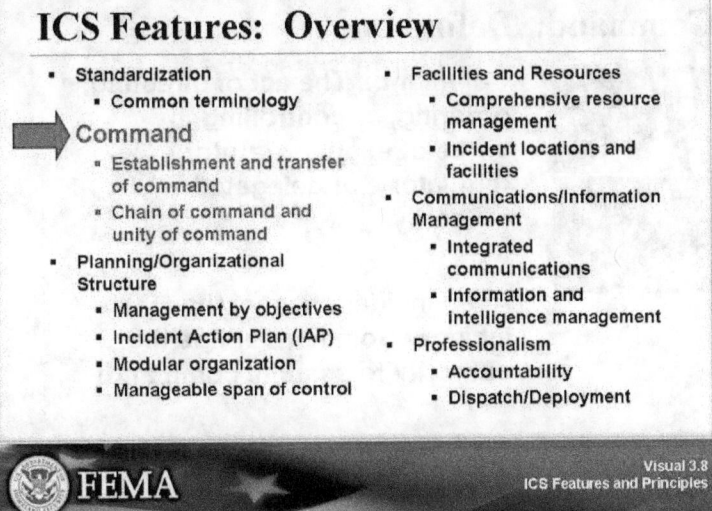

Visual Description: ICS Features Overview: Command

Instructor Notes

Tell the participants that the next part of this unit covers command, including:

- Establishment and transfer of command.
- Chain of command and unity of command.

| Topic | Command |

Visual 3.9

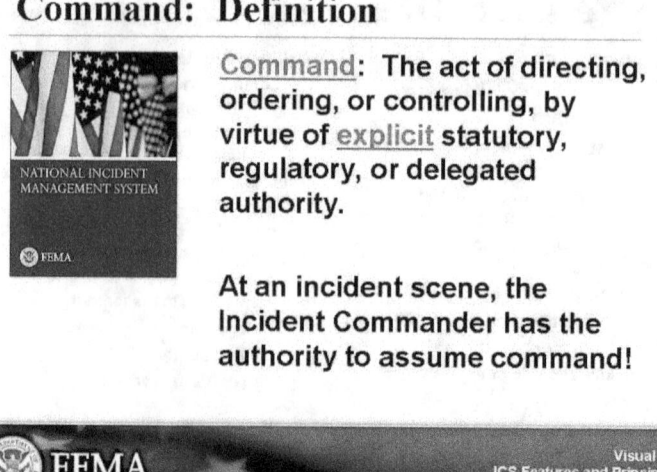

Command: Definition

Command: The act of directing, ordering, or controlling, by virtue of explicit statutory, regulatory, or delegated authority.

At an incident scene, the Incident Commander has the authority to assume command!

Visual 3.9
ICS Features and Principles

Visual Description: Command: Definition

Instructor Notes

Explain that NIMS defines command as the act of directing, ordering, or controlling by virtue of explicit statutory, regulatory, or delegated authority.

At an incident scene, the Incident Commander has the authority to assume command.

The Incident Commander should have the level of training, experience, and expertise to serve in this capacity. It is quite possible that the Incident Commander may not be the highest ranking official on scene.

| Topic | Command |

Visual 3.10

Transfer of Command

- Moves the responsibility for incident command from one Incident Commander to another.
- Must include a transfer of command briefing (which may be oral, written, or both).

FEMA

Visual 3.10
ICS Features and Principles

Visual Description: Transfer of Command

Instructor Notes

Tell the participants that the next ICS feature is transfer of command.

- The process of moving the responsibility for incident command from one Incident Commander to another is called transfer of command.

- The transfer of command process always includes a transfer of command briefing, which may be oral, written, or a combination of both.

- When a transfer of command takes place, it is important to announce the change to the rest of the incident staff.

Topic	Command

Visual 3.11

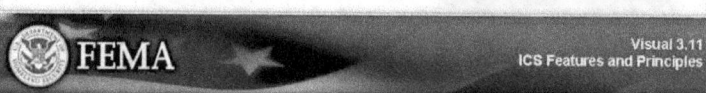

When Command Is Transferred

Command is transferred when:
- A more qualified Incident Commander arrives.
- A jurisdiction or agency is legally required to take command.
- Incident complexity changes.
- The current Incident Commander needs to rest.

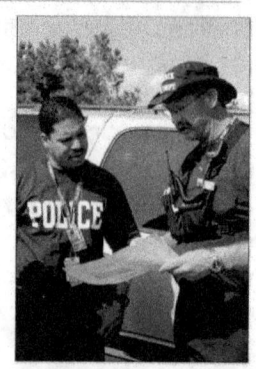

FEMA

Visual 3.11
ICS Features and Principles

Visual Description: When Command Is Transferred

Instructor Notes

Explain that there are several possible reasons that command might be transferred. Transfer of command may take place when:

- A more qualified Incident Commander arrives and assumes command. For example, a faculty member might act as the initial incident commander for an explosion in a science lab, but would then relinquish command to a more qualified Incident Commander when firefighters arrive.

- A jurisdiction or agency is legally required to take command. For example, the Federal Bureau of Investigation (FBI) is legally required to take the lead for investigations of terrorist incidents.

- The incident changes in complexity. For example, an incident might start on campus, but spread into the surrounding community, affecting multiple jurisdictions, institutions, or agencies.

- The current Incident Commander needs to rest. On long or extended incidents, there is normally turnover of personnel to accommodate work/rest requirements.

Topic	Command

Visual 3.12

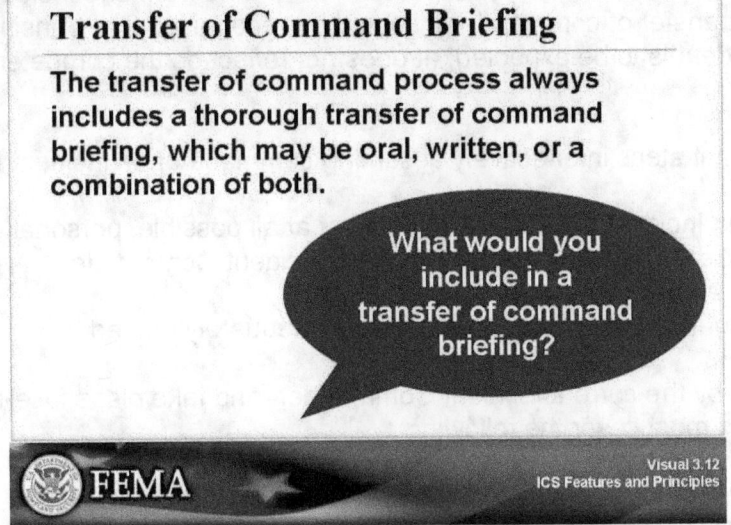

Visual Description: Transfer of Command Briefing

Instructor Notes

Explain that the transfer of command process always includes a thorough transfer of command briefing, which may be oral, written, or a combination of both.

It is also important to remember that the rest of the incident staff should be notified of the transfer of command.

What would you include in a transfer of command briefing?

→ Hint: Refer to the additional information on the next page!

Topic   **Transfer of Command**

The process of moving the responsibility for incident command from one Incident Commander to another is called "transfer of command." It should be recognized that transition of command on an expanding incident is to be expected. It does not reflect on the competency of the current Incident Commander.

There are five important steps in effectively assuming command of an incident in progress.

Step 1: The incoming Incident Commander should, if at all possible, personally perform an assessment of the incident situation with the existing Incident Commander.

Step 2: The incoming Incident Commander must be adequately briefed.

This briefing must be by the current Incident Commander, and take place face-to-face if possible. The briefing must cover the following:

- Incident history (what has happened)
- Priorities and objectives
- Current plan
- Resource assignments
- Incident organization
- Resources ordered/needed
- Facilities established
- Status of communications
- Any constraints or limitations
- Incident potential
- Delegation of authority

Step 3: After the incident briefing, the incoming Incident Commander should determine an appropriate time for transfer of command.

Step 4: At the appropriate time, notice of a change in incident command should be made to:
- Agency headquarters.
- General Staff members (if designated).
- Command Staff members (if designated).
- All incident personnel.

Step 5: The incoming Incident Commander may give the previous Incident Commander another assignment on the incident. There are several advantages to this strategy:

- The initial Incident Commander retains first-hand knowledge at the incident site.
- This strategy allows the initial Incident Commander to observe the progress of the incident and to gain experience.

Topic	Command

Visual 3.13

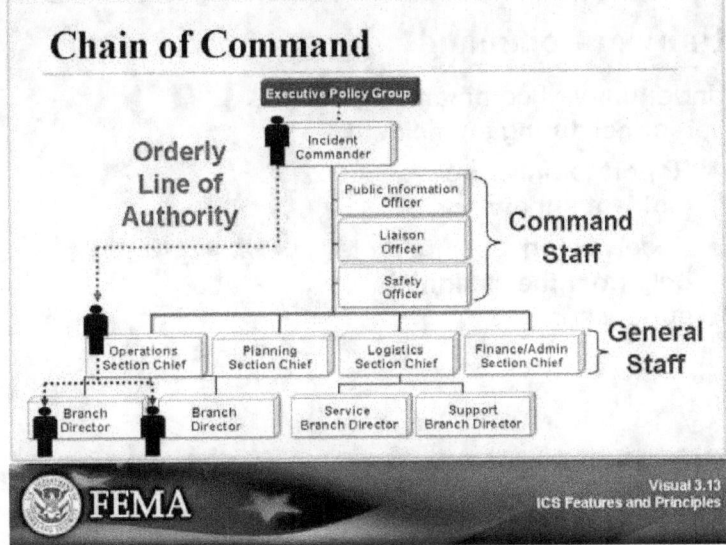

Visual Description: Chain of Command

Instructor Notes

Chain of command is an orderly line of authority within the ranks of the incident management organization. Chain of command:

- Allows incident managers to direct and control the actions of all personnel under their supervision.
- Avoids confusion by requiring that orders flow from supervisors.

Chain of command does not prevent personnel from directly communicating with each other to ask for or share information.

The features and principles used to manage an incident differ from day-to-day management approaches. Effective incident management relies on a tight command and control structure. Although information is exchanged freely through the ICS structure, strict adherence must be paid to top-down direction.

To make ICS work, each of us must commit to following this command and control approach.

Visual 3.14

Unity of Command

Under unity of command, personnel during an incident:

- Report to only <u>one</u> incident supervisor.
- Receive work assignments only from the assigned supervisor.

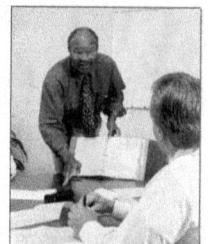

FEMA

Visual 3.14
ICS Features and Principles

Visual Description: Unity of Command

Instructor Notes

Under unity of command, personnel:

- Report to only one ICS supervisor.
- Receive work assignments only from their ICS supervisors.

| Topic | Command |

Visual 3.15

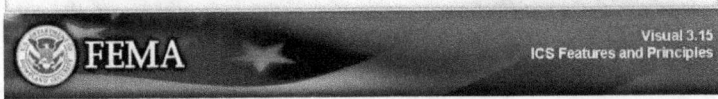

Incident Management Roles (1 of 2)

The Incident Commander's role is to:

- **Manage the incident at the scene.**
- **Keep officials in the Executive Policy Group informed on all important matters pertaining to the incident.**

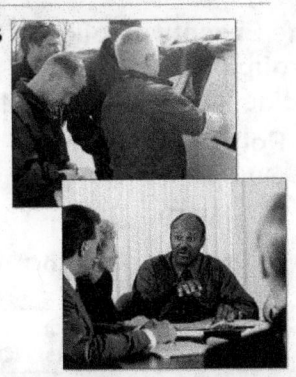

FEMA

Visual 3.15
ICS Features and Principles

Visual Description: Incident Management Roles – Incident Commander

---

Instructor Notes

The Incident Commander is the primary person in charge at the incident. In addition to managing the incident scene, he or she must keep officials in the Executive Policy Group informed and up to date on all important matters pertaining to the incident.

The ICS hierarchy of command must be maintained and not even executives and senior officials can bypass the system.

| Topic | Command |

Visual 3.16

Incident Management Roles (2 of 2)

The Executive Policy Group provides the Incident Commander with:

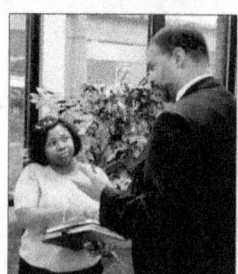

- Policy and Mission Guidance
- Overall Direction
- Delegation of Authority

To maintain the unity of command and safety of responders, the chain of command must NOT be bypassed.

FEMA

Visual 3.16
ICS Features and Principles

Visual Description: Incident Management Roles – Executive Policy Group

---

Instructor Notes

The executives/senior officials (Provost, Chancellor, President, etc.) are accountable for the incident. Along with this responsibility, by virtue of their position, these individuals have the authority to make policy decisions, commit resources, obligate funds, and obtain the resources necessary to protect the students and facilities. They delegate authority to the Incident Commander.

Having the responsibility does not mean that the Executive Policy Group assumes a command role over the on-scene incident operation. Rather, the Executive Policy Group:

- Provides policy guidance on priorities and objectives based on situational needs and the Emergency Operations Plan.
- Oversees resource coordination and support to the on-scene command from an Operations Center.

Instructor Note: Explain that ICS permits the Public Information Officer (PIO) to remain accountable to the Executive Policy Group for ensuring consistent, coordinated communications. However, the PIO must take direction from the Incident Commander at the scene. For example, on an incident involving a criminal investigation, the Incident Commander needs the authority to direct the PIO to keep the media out of the crime scene.

| Topic | Command |

Visual 3.17

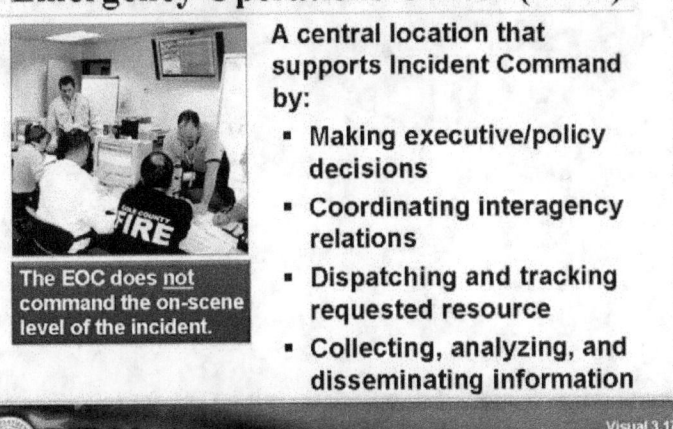

Visual Description: Emergency Operations Center (EOC)

Instructor Notes

Explain that Executive Policy Group may convene at the Emergency Operations Center (EOC).

Present the following key points:

An EOC is activated:
- To support the on-scene response during an escalating incident by relieving the burden of external coordination and securing additional resources.

An EOC is:
- A physical location.
- Staffed with personnel trained for and authorized to represent their agency/discipline.
- Equipped with mechanisms for communicating with the incident site and obtaining resources and potential resources.
- Managed through protocols.
- Applicable at different levels of government.

An EOC consists of:
- Personnel and equipment appropriate to the level of incident.

An EOC is used:
- In varying ways within all levels of government and the private sector.
- To provide coordination, direction, and support during emergencies.

An EOC does not:
- Command the on-scene level of the incident.

| Topic | Command |

Visual 3.18

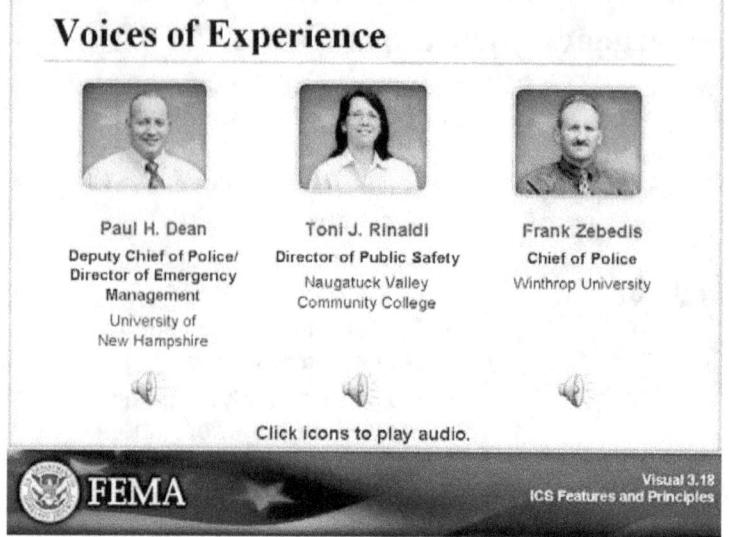

Visual Description: Voices of Experience

Instructor Notes

Tell the participants they will be hearing "voices of experience" from three campus personnel about the relationship between the Incident Commander and the Executive Policy Group.

Click on each icon to hear the "voice of experience."

Audio Transcripts:

Paul H. Dean
Deputy Chief of Police/Director of Emergency Management
University of New Hampshire

When it comes to the scene there, the Incident Commander is in charge of his or her scene on the ground; however, we all have a reporting line to report to. The CEO, the policy group, the EOC all require information to do their job and any Incident Commander knows that they're there to support his or her operation on the ground. Providing them accurate, timely information allows them to get you the things that you need to do to be successful on the ground. A properly, well-trained organization of people will know what their roles are. The president will know that he is, in the end, ultimately responsible for the safety on his college campus but he also knows that it's his job to trust his Incident Commander on the street that's making those decisions and those relationships need to be done well before an incident takes place and training such as this is the train that needed to be in place so that confidence is built and that people have those good conversations well in advance.

Audio Transcripts: (Continued)

Toni J Rinaldi
Director of Public Safety
Naugatuck Valley Community College

The Incident Commander is the person who takes control and command of the incident as the incident unfolds and that is the person that's in charge of the incident at the scene. On a college campus we cannot neglect the fact that our college president or provost or chancellor is obviously in charge of the campus and will never be asked to give that up; however, he or she will be in charge of the impact of the incident on the campus versus the incident itself.

Frank Zebedis
Chief of Police
Winthrop University

Well, the Executive Policy Group, they're responsible for managing what goes on at the institution. They're looking at the outcome: How they're going to get classes back in session? How are they going to get the word out? The Operations Section in a command post or in ICS—they're responsible for resolving the scene, the incident as it unfolds. They're not worried about how the president or how the executive officers are going to, you know, notify parents, how they're going to bring classes back in sessions or if they're going to cancel classes. Their responsibility is making sure that the scene is contained, the scene is resolved, and minimize as much damages as possible and to mitigate as much life loss or property loss as possible.

| Topic | Command |

Visual 3.19

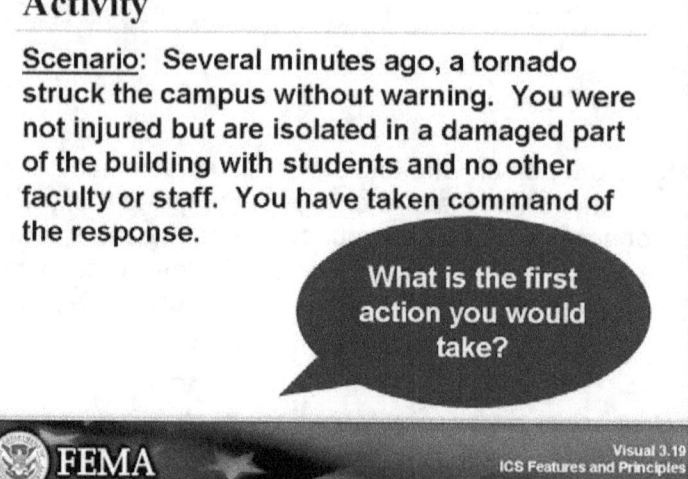

Visual Description: Activity: What is the first action that you would take?

Instructor Notes

Review the following scenario on assuming command:

> Scenario: Several minutes ago, a tornado struck the campus without warning. You were not injured but are isolated in a damaged part of the building with students and no other faculty or staff personnel. You have taken command of the response.
>
> **Question: What is the first action that you would take?**

Instructor Note: Use this scenario to transition to a discussion of incident objectives and action planning. If not mentioned by the students, note that the first actions would include sizing up the situation and taking measures to ensure life safety.

Topic	Planning/Organizational Structure

Visual 3.20

Visual Description: ICS Features Overview: Planning/Organizational Structure

Instructor Notes

Tell the participants that the next part of this lesson covers planning and organizational structure, including:

- Management by objectives.
- Incident Action Plan (IAP).
- Modular organization.
- Manageable span of control.

| Topic | Planning/Organizational Structure |

Visual 3.21

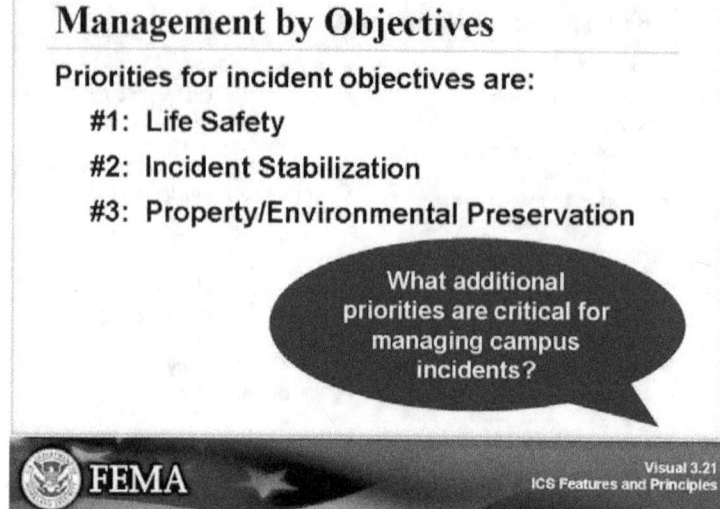

Visual Description: Management by Objectives

Instructor Notes

As educators, you understand the value of learning objectives. Incident objectives are used to ensure that everyone within the ICS organization has a clear understanding of what needs to be accomplished.

Priorities for incident objectives are:

1: Life Safety
2: Incident Stabilization
3: Property/Environmental Preservation

> **Ask the participants: What additional priorities are critical for managing campus incidents?**

Visual 3.22

ICS Organization

Differs from day-to-day organizational structures and positions by:

- Using unique ICS position titles and organizational structures.
- Assigning personnel based on expertise, not rank. For example, a director may not hold that title when deployed under an ICS structure.

FEMA

Visual 3.22
ICS Features and Principles

Visual Description: ICS Organization

Instructor Notes

The ICS organization is unique but easy to understand. There is no correlation between the ICS organization and the administrative structure of any single agency or jurisdiction. This is deliberate, because confusion over different position titles and organizational structures has been a significant stumbling block to effective incident management in the past.

For example, someone who serves as a director every day may not hold that title when deployed under an ICS structure.

Visual 3.23

Modular Organization

Incident command organizational structure is based on:

- Size, type, and complexity of the incident.
- Specifics of the hazard environment created by the incident.
- Incident planning process and incident objectives.

FEMA

Visual 3.23
ICS Features and Principles

Visual Description: Modular Organization

Instructor Notes

The ICS organizational structure develops in a top-down, modular fashion that is based on the size and complexity of the incident, as well as the specifics of the hazard environment created by the incident. As incident complexity increases, the organization expands from the top down as functional responsibilities are delegated.

The ICS organizational structure is flexible. When needed, separate functional elements can be established and subdivided to enhance internal organizational management and external coordination. As the ICS organizational structure expands, the number of management positions also expands to adequately address the requirements of the incident.

In a later unit, we'll look at how the Operations Section expands and contracts based on span of control.

Visual 3.24

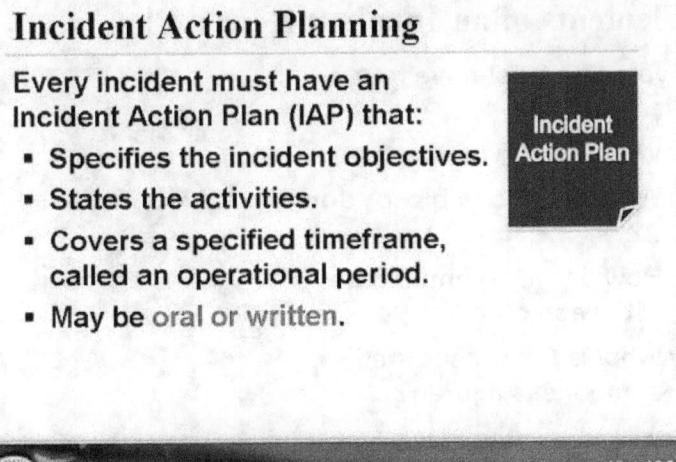

Visual Description: Incident Action Planning

Instructor Notes

Every response has a strategy—like a lesson plan—called an Incident Action Plan (IAP). The Incident Commander must ensure that the IAP:

- Specifies the incident objectives.
- States the activities to be completed.
- Covers a specified timeframe, called an operational period.
- May be **oral or written**—except for hazardous materials incidents, which require a written IAP.

Even the smallest of incidents are managed by incident objectives and plans. The plan can be as simple as the next steps the Incident Commander plans to do. The steps can be orally communicated to the rest of the ICS organization.

Visual 3.25

Elements of an Incident Action Plan

Every IAP must have four elements:

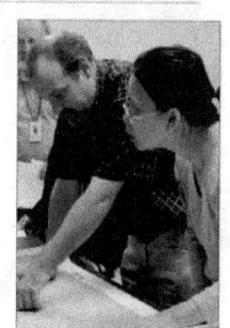

- What do we want to do?
- Who is responsible for doing it?
- How do we communicate with each other?
- What is the procedure if someone is injured?

FEMA

Visual 3.25
ICS Features and Principles

Visual Description: Elements of an Incident Action Plan

Instructor Notes

Explain that every IAP must answer the following four questions:

- What do we want to do?
- Who is responsible for doing it?
- How do we communicate with each other?
- What is the procedure if someone is injured?

Visual 3.26

Activity: Incident Action Plan

Instructions:
- Working as a team, identify four items you would include in an IAP for the computer worm scenario in Unit 2.
- Write these items on chart paper.
- Select a spokesperson. Be prepared to present in 5 minutes.

Scenario:
During freshman move-in, a dangerous worm has rapidly spread through the university computer system, consuming massive amounts of bandwidth, deleting files, and crippling the network.

FEMA

Visual 3.26
ICS Features and Principles

Visual Description: Activity: Incident Action Plan

Instructor Notes

Purpose: The purpose of this activity is to illustrate how to develop an IAP.

Instructions: Follow the steps below to conduct this activity:

1. Assign the participants to groups of five or six.
2. Explain that the participants should identify four items they would include in an Incident Action Plan for the computer worm scenario from Unit 2.
3. Tell the groups that they should record the IAP elements on chart paper and select a spokesperson to report back to the group.
4. Inform the groups that they will have 5 minutes to complete this activity.

Scenario: During freshman move-in, a dangerous worm has spread rapidly through the university computer network. The worm, which is consuming massive amounts of bandwidth, also includes a "payload" code designed to delete files on affected computers. The effects have essentially crippled the university computer network, including systems for course registration and emergency notification. The network is also used when students swipe their identification cards to enter residence halls and fitness facilities, and to pay for meals at campus dining halls. It remains unclear whether the incident poses a threat to sensitive information, such as student and employee Social Security numbers.

Debrief: Monitor the time. When 5 minutes have passed, ask the spokesperson from each group to present the elements of their IAP. Their answers should include:
- What they want to do.
- Who is responsible for doing it.
- How they will communicate with one another.
- The procedures if someone is injured.

Topic   **Planning/Organizational Structure**

Visual 3.27

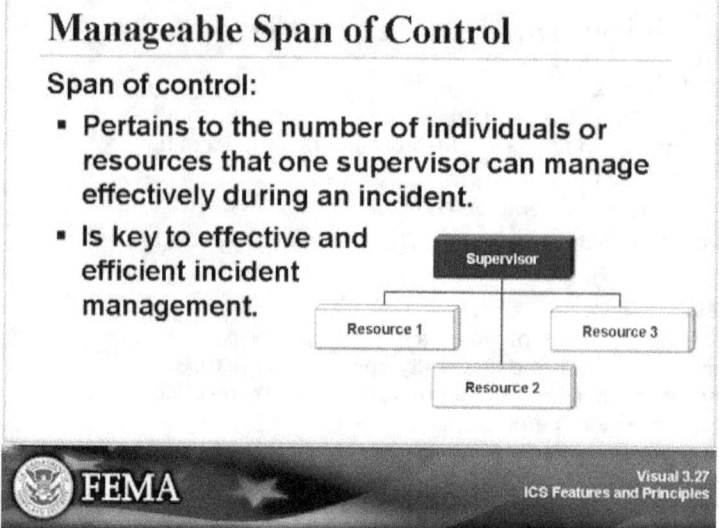

Visual Description: Manageable Span of Control

Instructor Notes

Tell the participants that another basic ICS feature concerns the supervisory structure of the organization. Maintaining adequate span of control throughout the ICS organization is very important.

Span of control pertains to the number of individuals or resources that one supervisor can manage effectively during an incident.

Maintaining an effective span of control is important at incidents where safety and accountability are a top priority.

Emphasize that supervisors must be able to adequately supervise and control their subordinates, as well as communicate with and manage all resources under their supervision.

| Topic | Planning/Organizational Structure |

Visual 3.28

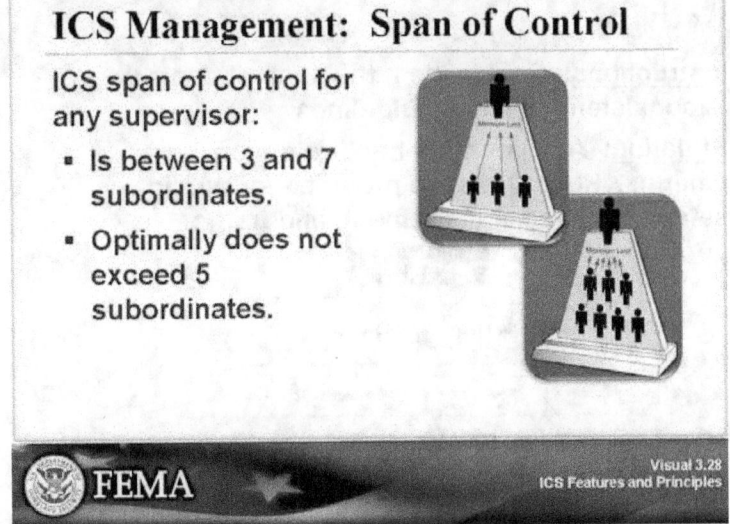

Visual Description: ICS Management: Span of Control

Instructor Notes

Review the following key points:

- Another basic ICS feature concerns the supervisory structure of the organization. Maintaining adequate span of control throughout the ICS organization is very important.

- Span of control pertains to the number of individuals or resources that one supervisor can manage effectively during an incident.

- The type of incident, nature of the task, hazards and safety factors, and distances between personnel and resources all influence span of control considerations. **Maintaining an effective span of control is particularly important on incidents where safety and accountability are a top priority.**

- Effective span of control on incidents may vary from three (3) to seven (7), and a ratio of one (1) supervisor to five (5) reporting elements is recommended.

Ask the participants: What types of incidents warrant a low span-of-control ratio?

Visual 3.29

Activity

Instructions: Determine if the span of control is consistent with ICS guidelines.

Situation: A water main has broken on campus. Resources are provided for public safety, facilities management, and traffic control.

Incident Command

Resource | Resource | Resource | Resource

Resource | Resource | Resource | Resource

FEMA

Visual 3.29
ICS Features and Principles

Visual Description: Activity

Instructor Notes

Tell the participants to review the situation on the visual.

Situation: A water main has broken on campus. Resources are provided for public safety, facilities management, and traffic control.

Ask the participants to determine if the span of control is consistent with ICS guidelines.

Allow the participants time to respond.

If not mentioned, point out that the span of control is NOT consistent with ICS guidelines. Remind them that ICS span of control for any supervisor is between 3 and 7 subordinates and optimally does not exceed 5 subordinates.

| Topic | Facilities and Resources |

Visual 3.30

Visual Description: ICS Features Overview: Facilities and Resources

Instructor Notes

Tell the participants that the next part of this unit covers facilities and resources, including:

- Comprehensive resource management.
- Incident locations and facilities.

| Topic | Video: Incident Facilities Virtual Tour |

Visual 3.31

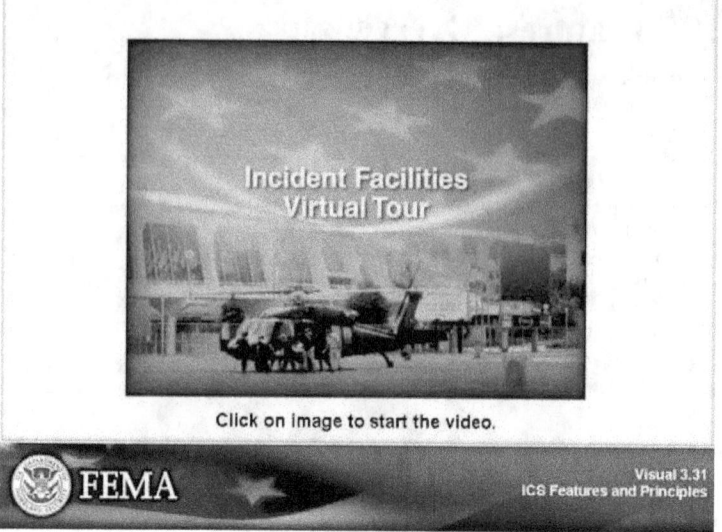

Visual Description: Video: Incident Facilities Virtual Tour

Instructor Notes

Present the following key points:

- Incident activities may be accomplished from a variety of operational locations and support facilities.

- The Incident Commander identifies and establishes needed facilities depending on incident needs. Standardized names are used to identify types of facilities.

- In order to integrate with community responders, it is important to be familiar with the standard ICS facilities.

- Some or all of these facilities may be used in some campus incidents and in other incidents in the community.

Video Transcript:

This presentation introduces the ICS facilities. In less complex incidents you most likely will not need many of the standard ICS facilities. However, in large incidents, such as Hurricane Katrina, undamaged campuses are often converted into ICS facilities.

(Continued on next page.)

Video Transcript (Continued):

The Incident Command Post, or ICP, is the location from which the Incident Commander oversees all incident operations. There is generally only one ICP for each incident, but it may change locations during the event. Every incident must have some form of an Incident Command Post. The ICP may be located outside; in a vehicle, trailer, or tent; or within a building. The ICP will be positioned outside of the present and potential hazard zone but close enough to the incident to maintain command.

Staging Areas are temporary locations at an incident where personnel and equipment wait to be assigned. Staging Areas should be located close enough to the incident for a timely response, but far enough away to be out of the immediate impact zone. In large complex incidents, there may be more than one Staging Area at an incident. Staging Areas can be collocated with other ICS facilities.

A Base is the location from which primary logistics and administrative functions are coordinated and administered.

A Camp is the location where resources may be kept to support incident operations if a Base is not accessible to all resources. Camps are equipped and staffed to provide food, water, sleeping areas, and sanitary services. A gym or dining hall could be used as a Camp for a community-wide incident.

A Helibase is the location from which helicopter-centered air operations are conducted. Helibases are generally used on a more long-term basis and include such services as fueling and maintenance.

Helispots are more temporary locations at the incident, where helicopters can safely land and take off. Multiple Helispots may be used. Think about your campus. Could you use a parking lot or athletic field for a temporary Helispot?

Let's review the different ICS facilities covered in this video.

- The **Incident Command Post** is the location from which the Incident Commander oversees all incident operations.
- **Staging Areas** are where personnel and equipment are gathered while waiting to be assigned.
- A **Base** is the location from which primary logistics and administrative functions are coordinated and administered.
- A **Helibase** is the location from which helicopter-centered air operations are conducted.
- **Helispots** are more temporary locations at the incident, where helicopters can safely land and take off.

| Topic | Facilities and Resources |

Visual 3.32

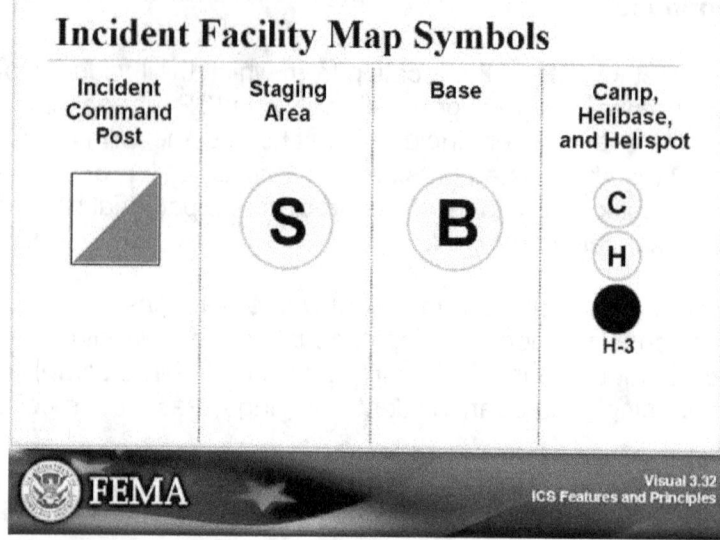

Visual Description: Incident Facility Map Symbols

Instructor Notes

Explain that in ICS, it is important to be able to identify the map symbols associated with the basic incident facilities.

The map symbols used to represent each of the six basic ICS facilities are shown in the illustration.

Ask the participants the following question:

Helicopters were taking off and landing at a football field after a tornado severely damaged the campus. What map symbol would indicate this ICS facility?

If not mentioned by the group, explain that the ICS facility could be a Helibase or Helispot and point out the symbols in the visual.

Have you pre-identified locations for incident facilities?

| Topic | Facilities and Resources |

Visual 3.33

Incident Facilities: Summary

- A single Incident Command Post should be established on all incidents—even small ones!
- Campus incidents may require additional facilities (e.g., a student call center).
- Areas on campus may be predesignated incident facilities for the surrounding community (e.g., shelters, staging areas, helibases, medical centers).

FEMA

Visual 3.33
ICS Features and Principles

Visual Description: ICS Facilities: Summary

Instructor Notes

Present the following points:

- A single Incident Command Post should be established on all incidents, even on a small incident.

- Campus incidents may require additional facilities beyond those that are standard ICS facilities.

Example: For example, if you need a Student-Parent Reunification Area, a Media Center, or a Call Center for students to use, add those sites to your incident facilities. It is preferable to add needed facilities rather than to use a standard ICS facility, such as a Staging Area, for a campus-unique function. A Staging Area is intended only for responders waiting for assignments, not parents waiting for their students.

Note that higher education institutions often play a support role in the community, and areas on campus might be predesignated as incident facilities for the surrounding area. This might include medical centers, shelters, helibases, staging areas, and storage for historic artifacts/archives.

Do you know if areas of your campus have been designated as incident facilities for the surrounding community?

| Topic | Facilities and Resources |

Visual 3.34

Resources: Definition

Resources are personnel and major items of equipment, supplies, and facilities available or potentially available for assignment to incident operations and for which status is maintained.

FEMA

Visual 3.34
ICS Features and Principles

Visual Description: Resources: Definition

Instructor Notes

Explain that, in ICS, resources include personnel and major items of equipment, supplies, and facilities available or potentially available for assignment to incident operations and for which status is maintained.

| Topic | Facilities and Resources |

Visual 3.35

Resource Management

Resource management includes processes for:

- Categorizing resources.
- Ordering resources.
- Dispatching resources.
- Tracking resources.
- Recovering resources.
- Reimbursing other organizations, as appropriate.

FEMA

Visual 3.35
ICS Features and Principles

Visual Description: Resource Management

Instructor Notes

Note that as mentioned in the previous unit, resources at an incident must be managed effectively. Maintaining an accurate and up-to-date picture of resource utilization is a critical component of incident management. Resource management includes processes for:

- Categorizing, credentialing, and pre-identifying resources.
- Ordering resources.
- Dispatching resources.
- Tracking resources.
- Recovering resources.

Point out that resource management also includes processes for reimbursement for resources, as appropriate.

Explain that **credentialing** is providing documentation that can authenticate and verify the certification and identity of designated incident managers and emergency responders.

| Topic | Facilities and Resources |

Visual 3.36

Activity

Instructions: Review the following scenario and answer the questions that follow.

Scenario: During finals week, a fire burns down an academic building on campus. The cause of the fire is unknown, although arson is suspected.

Question: Where on your campus would you establish a staging area?

FEMA

Visual 3.36
ICS Features and Principles

Visual Description: Activity

Instructor Notes

Tell the participants to review the scenario and answer the question that follows.

Scenario: During finals week, a fire burns down an academic building on campus. The cause of the fire is unknown, although arson is suspected.

Question: Where on your campus would you establish a Staging Area?

Instructor Note: Allow participants time to respond. There is no single correct response. If not mentioned by course participants, note that the location of the Staging Area should take into consideration factors such as access, site security, and communications.

| Topic | Communications/Information Management |

Visual 3.37

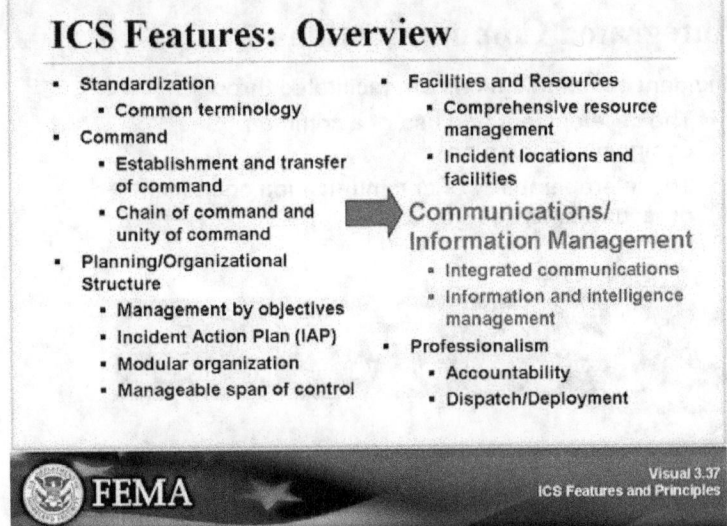

Visual Description: ICS Features Overview: Communications/Information Management

---

Instructor Notes

Tell the participants that the next part of this unit covers communications and information management, including:

- Integrated communications.
- Information and intelligence management.

Visual 3.38

Integrated Communications

Incident communications are facilitated through:

- The development and use of a common communications plan.
- The interoperability of communication equipment, procedures, and systems.

Before an incident, it is critical to develop an integrated voice and data communications system (equipment, systems, and protocols).

FEMA

Visual 3.38
ICS Features and Principles

Visual Description: Integrated Communications

Instructor Notes

Present the following points:

- A common communications plan is essential for ensuring that responders can communicate with one another during an incident.

- The response to the Columbine school shooting incident was hampered by response agencies operating on radios set to different frequencies.

- Prior to an incident, higher education institutions must work with local responders to ensure that communications equipment, procedures, and systems can operate together during a response (interoperable).

Topic	Communications/Information Management

Visual 3.39

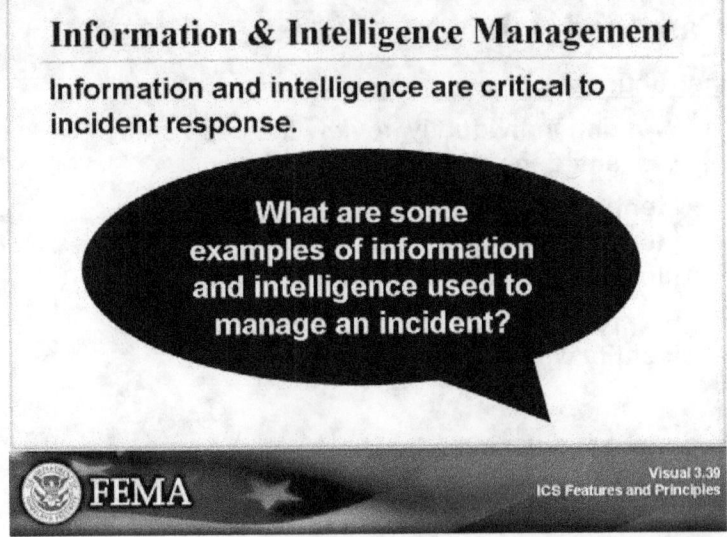

Visual Description: Information & Intelligence Management: What are some examples of information and intelligence used to manage an incident?

Instructor Notes

Note that the analysis and sharing of information and intelligence is an important component of ICS. Incident management must establish a process for gathering, sharing, and managing incident-related information and intelligence.

Ask the participants the following question:

What are some examples of information and intelligence used to manage an incident?

If not mentioned by the participants, add the following items:

Intelligence includes other operational information that may come from a variety of different sources, such as:

- Weather forecasts.
- Upcoming student activities and planned events.
- Structural plans and vulnerabilities.
- Risk assessments.
- Threats including potential for campus violence.
- Surveillance of disease outbreak.

Visual 3.40

Case Study: Incident Management

Instructions:

1. Working individually, review the case study presented in your Student Manuals.

2. Identify the lessons learned from the incident that you would apply to managing incident information and intelligence.

3. Be prepared to discuss the lessons you identify with the class in 5 minutes.

FEMA

Visual 3.40
ICS Features and Principles

Visual Description: Case Study: Incident Management

Instructor Notes

Tell the participants to read the scenario below and identify lessons learned from the scenario that they would apply to managing incident information and intelligence. Note that although this scenario took place at a high school, the lessons learned are nonetheless important for all educational institutions.

Scenario: At the Columbine school shooting incident, police and emergency response crews arrived within minutes of 911 calls. One of the first functions of a SWAT incident is to acquire intelligence. The SWAT team commander found some students, who quickly sketched a layout of the school. As the situation evolved, officers received a lot of false information including: there were as many as eight gunmen, snipers were on the roof, and killers were hiding in ceilings or in heating ducts or trying to mingle with escaping students. The lack of reliable information hampered the operation.

If not mentioned by the group, present the sample answers shown below:

- Assign someone to serve as a point of contact with arriving responders to brief them on information about the campus layout and facilities.
- Prior to incidents, ensure that first responders have copies of maps, floor plans, and other critical information about the campus.
- Ensure that communications systems used by campus personnel and first responders are interoperable, so everyone can communicate with each other.
- Establish a single Incident Command Post so that you can work with first responders to jointly analyze and verify information.

| Topic | Professionalism |

Visual 3.41

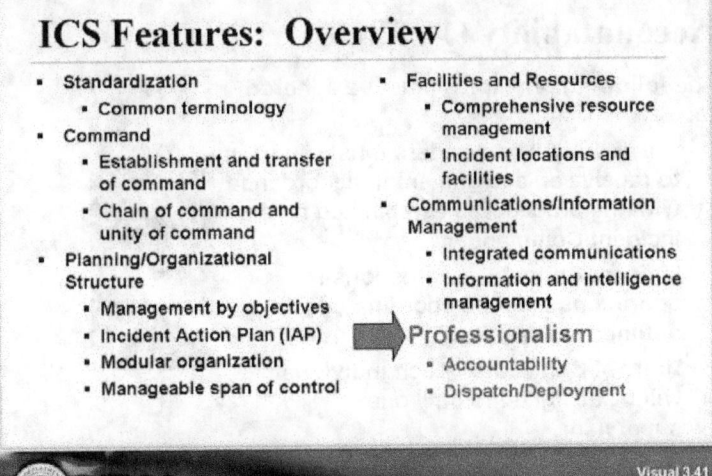

Visual Description: ICS Features Overview: Professionalism

Instructor Notes

Tell the participants that the last part of this unit covers professionalism, including:

- Accountability.
- Dispatch/deployment.

Visual 3.42

Accountability (1 of 2)

The following principles must be adhered to:

- Check-In. All responders must report in to receive an assignment in accordance with the procedures established by the Incident Commander.
- Incident Action Plan. Response operations must be coordinated as outlined in the IAP.
- Unity of Command. Each individual will be assigned to only one supervisor.

FEMA

Visual 3.42
ICS Features and Principles

Visual Description: Accountability (1 of 2)

Instructor Notes

Explain that effective accountability during incident operations is essential. Point out that individuals must abide by their institutional policies and guidelines and any applicable local, State, or Federal rules and regulations.

Explain that the following principles must be adhered to:

- **Check-In.** All responders must report in to receive an assignment in accordance with the procedures established by the Incident Commander.

- **Incident Action Plan.** Response operations must be coordinated as outlined in the IAP.

- **Unity of Command.** Each individual will be assigned to only one supervisor.

The next visual includes additional principles that must be adhered to.

| Topic | Professionalism |

Visual 3.43

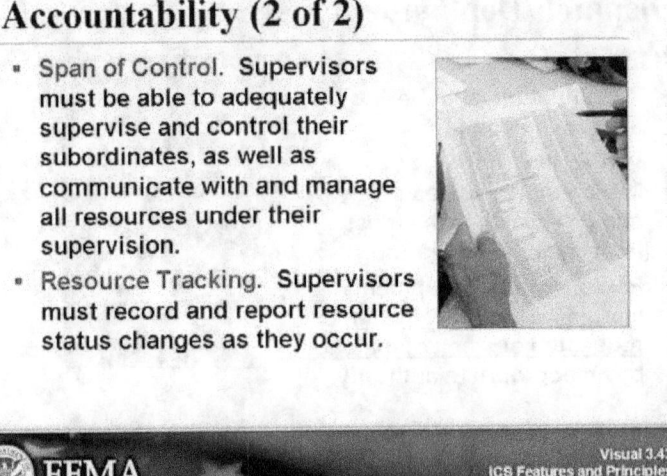

Visual Description: Accountability (2 of 2)

Instructor Notes

Continue by explaining that the following principles must be adhered to:

- **Span of Control.** Supervisors must be able to adequately supervise and control their subordinates, as well as communicate with and manage all resources under their supervision.

- **Resource Tracking.** Supervisors must record and report resource status changes as they occur.

Visual 3.44

Dispatch/Deployment

At any incident:

- The situation must be assessed and the response planned.
- Managing resources safely and effectively is the most important consideration.
- Personnel and equipment <u>should respond only when requested or when dispatched</u> by an appropriate authority.

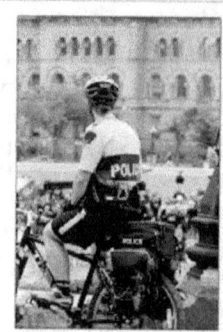

FEMA

Visual 3.44
ICS Features and Principles

Visual Description: Dispatch/Deployment

Instructor Notes

Point out that another key feature of ICS is the importance of managing resources to adjust to changing conditions.

When an incident occurs, you must be dispatched or deployed to become part of the incident response. In other words, until you are deployed to the incident organization, you remain in your everyday role.

After being deployed, your **first task is to check in and receive an assignment**.

Emphasize that as campus personnel, you should be mobilized or activated to join the incident response. Unless you must take an immediate life-saving action, you should not start responding without being deployed. The deployment process improves safety and cuts down on chaos.

After check-in, you will locate your incident supervisor and obtain your initial briefing. The briefings you receive and give should include:

- Current assessment of the situation.
- Identification of your specific job responsibilities.
- Identification of coworkers.
- Location of work area.
- Identification of break areas, as appropriate.
- Procedural instructions for obtaining needed resources.
- Operational periods/work shifts.
- Required **safety procedures** and Personal Protective Equipment (PPE), as appropriate.

| Topic | Professionalism |

Visual 3.45

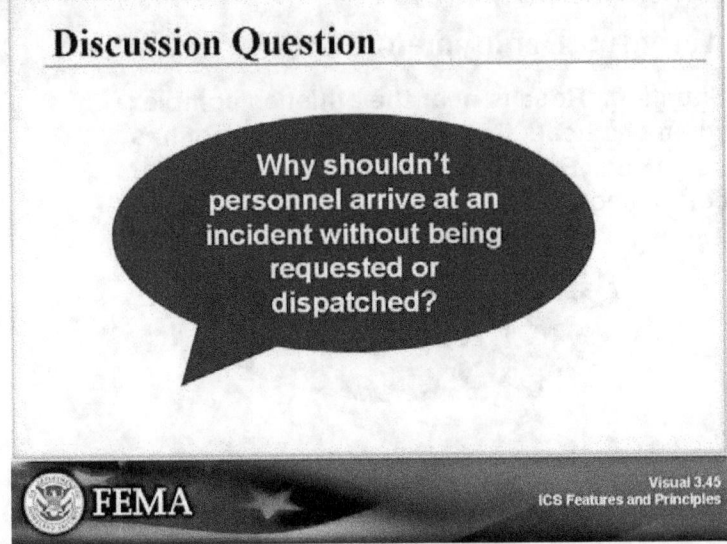

Visual Description: Discussion Question: Why shouldn't personnel arrive at an incident without being requested or dispatched?

Instructor Notes

Ask the participants the following discussion question:

Why shouldn't personnel arrive at an incident without being requested or dispatched?

If not mentioned by the participants, add the following points:

- Uncontrolled and uncoordinated arrival of resources at emergencies causes significant accountability issues.
- Self-dispatched or freelancing resources cause safety risks to responders, civilians, and others who are operating within the parameters of the Incident Action Plan.
- Chaos at the scene occurs, creating additional risks.
- Emergency access routes can be blocked, preventing trained responders from gaining access to the site or not allowing critically injured personnel to be transported from the scene.

In the World Trade Center 9/11 response, many responders self-dispatched, undermining command and control at the scene and clogging the streets so that other responders assigned to the WTC had difficulty getting through.

The bottom line is that when resources show up that have not been requested, the incident management system may fail.

| Topic | Professionalism |

Visual 3.46

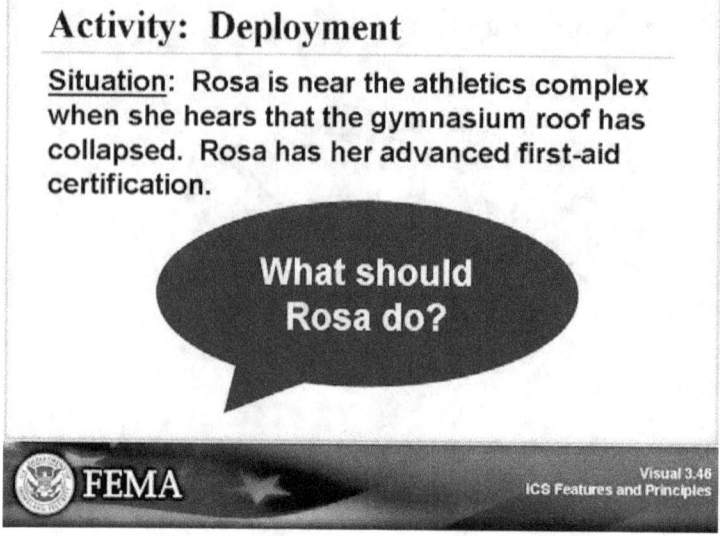

Visual Description: Activity: Deployment

Instructor Notes

Review the following situation: Rosa is near the athletics complex when she hears that the gymnasium roof has collapsed. Rosa has her advanced first-aid certification.

Ask the participants: What should Rosa do?

Elicit input from the participants. If not mentioned by the participants, explain that Rosa should report her whereabouts to the incident management team and wait for deployment to the scene. Rosa should not immediately rush to the scene.

| Topic | Summary |

Visual 3.47

Visual Description: Summary (1 of 2)

Instructor Notes

Review the key points on the visual.

ICS:

- Utilizes management features including the use of common terminology and a modular organizational structure.

- Emphasizes effective planning through the use of management by objectives and Incident Action Plans.

- Supports responders by providing data they need through effective information and intelligence management.

| Topic | Summary |

Visual 3.48

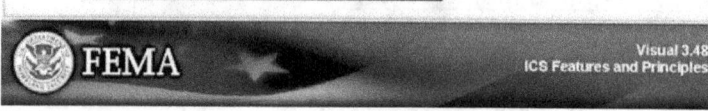

Summary (2 of 2)

ICS:

- Utilizes the principles of <u>chain of command</u>, <u>unity of command</u>, and <u>transfer of command</u>.

- Ensures full utilization of incident resources by maintaining a <u>manageable span of control</u>, establishing predesignated <u>incident facilities</u>, implementing <u>resource management</u> practices, and ensuring <u>integrated communications</u>.

FEMA
Visual 3.48
ICS Features and Principles

Visual Description: Summary (2 of 2)

Instructor Notes

Review the key points on the visual.

ICS:

- Utilizes the principles of chain of command, unity of command, and transfer of command.

- Ensures full utilization of incident resources by maintaining a manageable span of control, establishing predesignated incident facilities, implementing resource management practices, and ensuring integrated communications.

Ask if anyone has any questions about content covered in this unit.

Transition to the next unit by explaining that Unit 4 will cover the Incident Commander and Command Staff functions.

Your Notes:

Unit 4: Incident Commander and Command Staff Functions

Objectives

At the end of this unit, the participants should be able to:

- Identify the five major ICS management functions.
- Describe the role and function of the Incident Commander.
- Describe the role and function of the Command Staff.

Scope

- Unit Introduction
- Unit Objectives
- Management Functions
- Incident Commander
  - Establishing Command
  - Audio Clips: Voices of Experience
  - Delegating Incident Management Functions
  - Audio Clip: Incident Commander Role
  - Incident Commander Responsibilities
  - Audio Clip: Incident Commander Responsibilities
  - Deputy Incident Commander
- Command Staff
  - Expanding the Organization
  - Public Information Officer (PIO)
  - Safety Officer
  - Liaison Officer
  - Audio Clips: Meet the Command Staff
  - Command Staff Qualifications
- Activity: Command Staff Roles
- Summary

Methodology

The instructors will outline the objectives for this unit. The instructors will overview the management functions that are part of every incident, and will then overview the role of the Incident Commander. The participants will listen to an audio clip in which an Incident Commander talks about his role. Next, the instructors will summarize the Incident Commander's responsibilities. The participants will then listen to another audio clip in which an Incident Commander talks about responsibilities. After the audio clip, the instructors will introduce the role of the Deputy Incident Commander.

(Continued on next page.)

Methodology (Continued)

Next, the instructors will transition to the Command Staff. The presentation outlines the responsibilities of the Public Information Officer, Safety Officer, and Liaison Officer. The participants will listen to three audio clips in which members of the Command Staff speak.

The instructors will then lead an activity in which the participants apply the roles of the Command Staff to a scenario. To summarize the unit, the instructors will review the unit objectives and then transition to Unit 5.

Time Plan

A suggested time plan for this unit is shown below. More or less time may be required, based on the experience level of the group.

Topic	Time
Unit Introduction and Unit Objectives	5 minutes
Management Functions	5 minutes
Incident Commander	15 minutes
Command Staff	15 minutes
Activity: Command Staff Roles	15 minutes
Summary	5 minutes
Total Time	**1 hour**

| Topic | Unit Introduction |

Visual 4.1

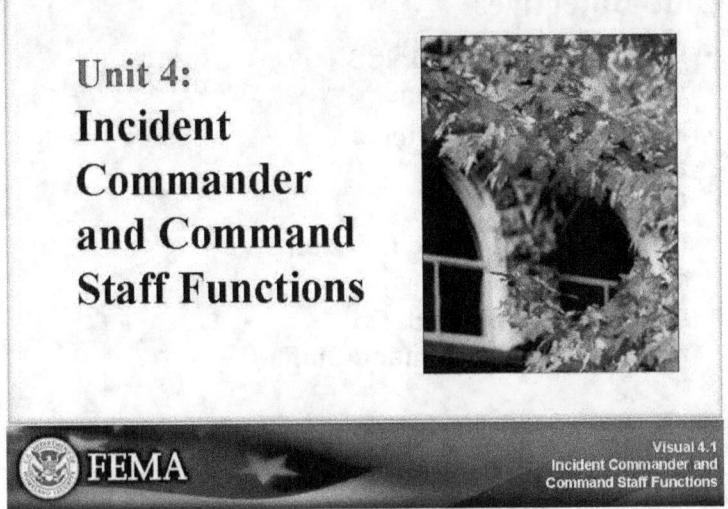

Visual Description: Unit Introduction

Instructor Notes

Tell the group that this unit will provide an overview of the role of the Incident Commander and Command Staff, including these topics:

- Five major management functions
- Incident Commander roles and responsibilities
- Command Staff roles and responsibilities

| Topic | Unit Objectives |

Visual 4.2

Unit Objectives

- Identify the five major ICS management functions.
- Identify the position titles associated with the Command Staff.
- Describe the role and function of the Incident Commander.
- Describe the role and function of the Command Staff.

FEMA

Visual 4.2
Incident Commander and
Command Staff Functions

Visual Description: Unit Objectives

Instructor Notes

Tell the group that by the end of this unit they should be able to:

- Identify the five major ICS management functions.
- Identify the position titles associated with the Command Staff.
- Describe the role and function of the Incident Commander.
- Describe the role and function of the Command Staff.

Visual 4.3

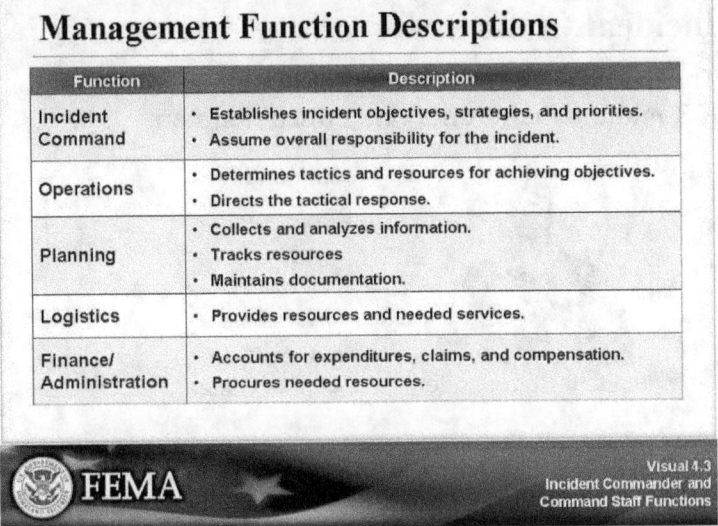

Visual Description: Management Function Descriptions

Instructor Notes

Present the following points:

Every incident requires that certain management functions be performed. The problem must be identified and assessed, a plan to deal with it developed and implemented, and the necessary resources procured and paid for.

Regardless of the size of the incident, these management functions still will apply.

There are five major management functions that are the foundation upon which the ICS organization develops. These functions include:

Incident Command   Sets the incident objectives, strategies, and priorities and has overall responsibility for the incident.

Operations   Conducts operations to reach the incident objectives. Establishes the tactics and directs all operational resources.

Planning   Supports the incident action planning process by tracking resources, collecting/analyzing information, and maintaining documentation.

Logistics   Provides resources and needed services to support the achievement of the incident objectives.

Finance & Administration   Monitors costs related to the incident. Provides accounting, procurement, time recording, and cost analyses.

| Topic | Incident Commander |

Visual 4.4

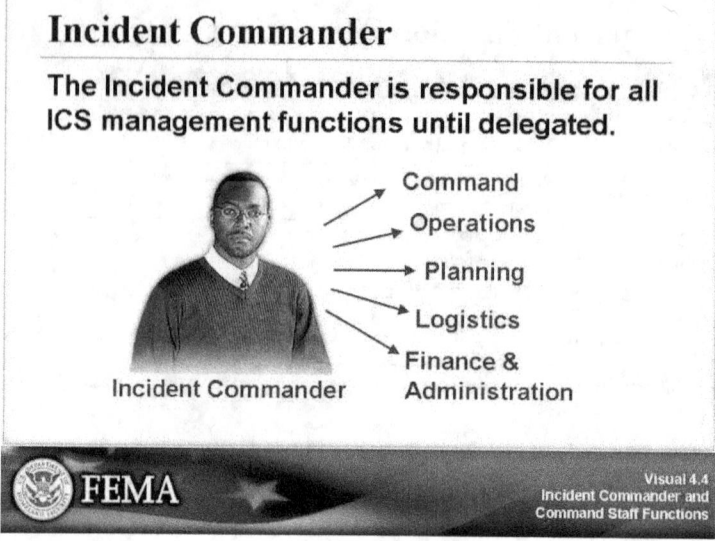

Visual Description: Incident Commander

___

Instructor Notes

___

Explain that the Incident Commander has overall responsibility for managing the incident by establishing objectives, planning strategies, and implementing tactics.

Emphasize that the **Incident Commander is the only position that is always staffed in ICS applications.** On small incidents and events, one person, the Incident Commander, may accomplish all management functions.

Remind the participants that the Incident Commander is responsible for all ICS management functions until he or she delegates the function.

Visual 4.5

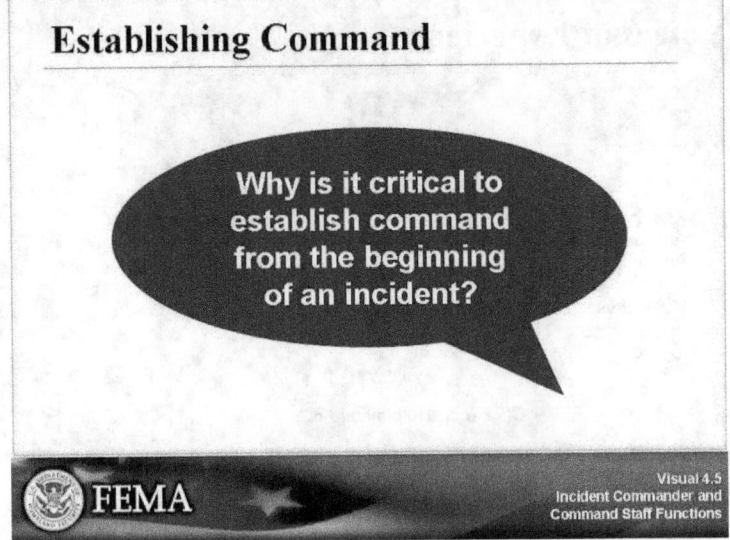

Visual Description: Establishing Command: Why is it critical to establish command from the beginning of an incident?

Instructor Notes

Ask the participants the following question:

Why is it critical to establish command from the beginning of an incident?

If not mentioned by the participants, add the following key points:

- Lack of command becomes a safety hazard for responders, students, and staff.
- Sizeup and decisionmaking are impossible without a command structure.
- It is difficult to expand a disorganized organization if the incident escalates.

Emphasize that all incident responses begin by establishing command.

| Topic | Incident Commander |

Visual 4.6

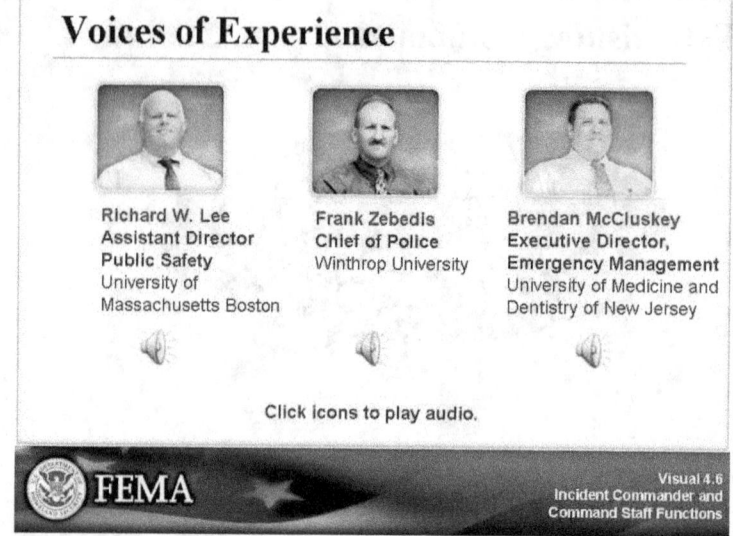

Visual Description: Voices of Experience

Instructor Notes

Tell the participants they will be hearing "voices of experience" from campus personnel about the role of the Incident Commander in campus incidents.

Click on each icon to hear the "voice of experience."

Audio Transcripts:

Richard W. Lee
Assistant Director of Public Safety
University of Massachusetts Boston

Who's in charge? Well, that's a complex question. It'll depend on the incident. It'll depend on the location. It'll depend on the jurisdiction. There's a lot of things that come into it but basically the best qualified person who's at the scene when the incident becomes, starts will be in charge and then it will move up the line as more qualified or better qualified or other people show up on the scene. It's very flexible in that respect and ICS and who's in charge doesn't, it's more of a function than it is a person. It's going to be the best person to do the job at the time as opposed to looking around for an arbitrary figure that has a title.

Audio Transcripts: (Continued)

Frank Zebedis
Chief of Police
Winthrop University

Who's in charge initially, on the onset of an incident, it could be the first, first responder which could be a professor; it could be a faculty member, a staff member, a coach, a citizen, or the first emergency responder who shows up on the scene is in charge, but as the event grows and more qualified people arrive to the scene, whoever is in charge then gets passed off to the more qualified person till eventually you have yourself an Incident Commander who is in position to manage the scene but until that time it takes a while for these responders to get there. It doesn't happen in a matter of seconds or minutes, so that initial person is actually in charge until the scene grows.

Brendan McCluskey
Executive Director, Emergency Management
University of Medicine and Dentistry of New Jersey

The Incident Commander is in charge and that's a principle of ICS that makes it clear who has the authority or who has the responsibility for overseeing what goes on at an incident scene, and regardless of where you come from, whether you are from the outside or the inside of the institution, whether you are police or fire or public works or public health or student services, the Incident Commander is the one who is going to be running the show. So it doesn't really matter where you're from, what your title is, what level of responsibility you have on a day-to-day basis, once you become part of that incident response, then you look up to that Incident Commander to be the one who is in charge.

Topic   **Incident Commander**

Visual 4.7

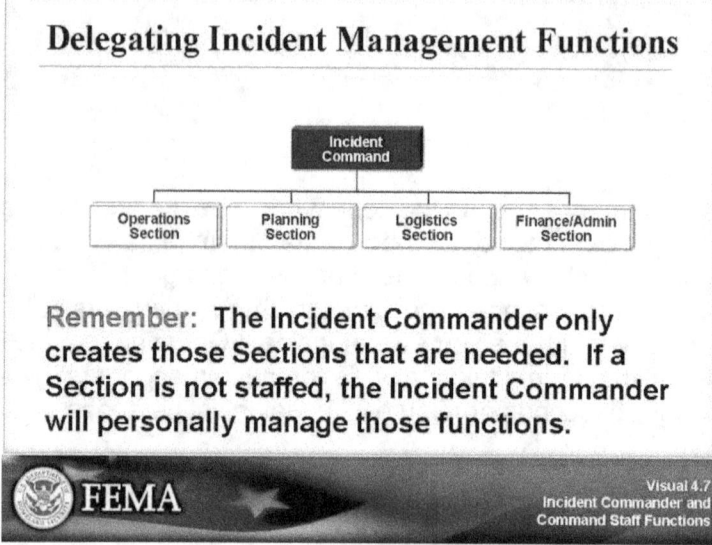

Visual Description: Delegating Incident Management Functions

Instructor Notes

Remind the participants that the ICS organization is modular and has the capability to expand or contract to meet the needs of the incident. On a larger incident, the Incident Commander may create Sections and delegate the Operations, Planning, Logistics, and Finance/Administration functions.

| Topic | Incident Commander |

Visual 4.8

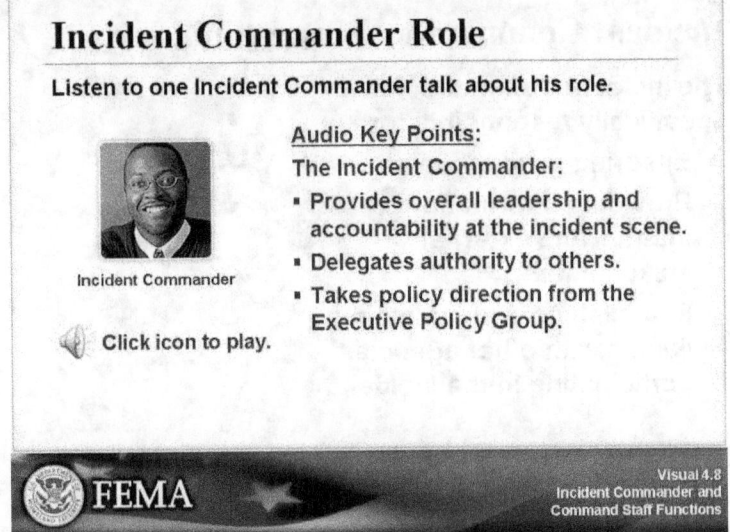

Visual Description: Incident Commander Role

Instructor Notes

Tell the group that they will now listen to an audio clip in which an Incident Commander talks about his role.

To play the audio, click on the icon. The total running time for this clip is 26 seconds.

Audio Transcript:

My job is to provide the overall leadership and accountability at the incident scene. I am able to delegate my authority to others to manage the ICS organization. I take policy direction and receive support from the Executive Policy Group. However, at the incident scene, I am in charge.

Visual 4.9

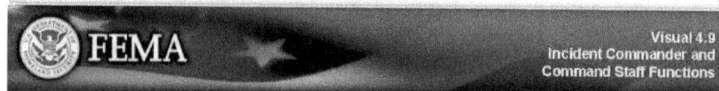

Incident Commander Responsibilities

The Incident Commander is specifically responsible for:

- Ensuring incident safety.
- Providing information to internal and external stakeholders.
- Establishing and maintaining liaison with other agencies participating in the incident.

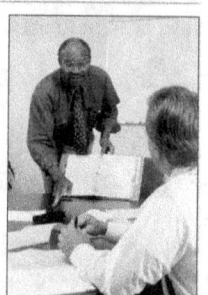

FEMA

Visual 4.9
Incident Commander and
Command Staff Functions

Visual Description: Incident Commander Responsibilities

Instructor Notes

Explain that the Incident Commander is specifically responsible for:

- Ensuring incident safety.
- Providing information to internal and external stakeholders.
- Establishing and maintaining liaison with other agencies participating in the incident.

Note that these are critical functions and, until delegated, are the responsibility of the Incident Commander.

The Incident Commander may appoint one or more Deputies. **Deputy Incident Commanders must be as qualified as the Incident Commander.**

| Topic | Incident Commander |

Visual 4.10

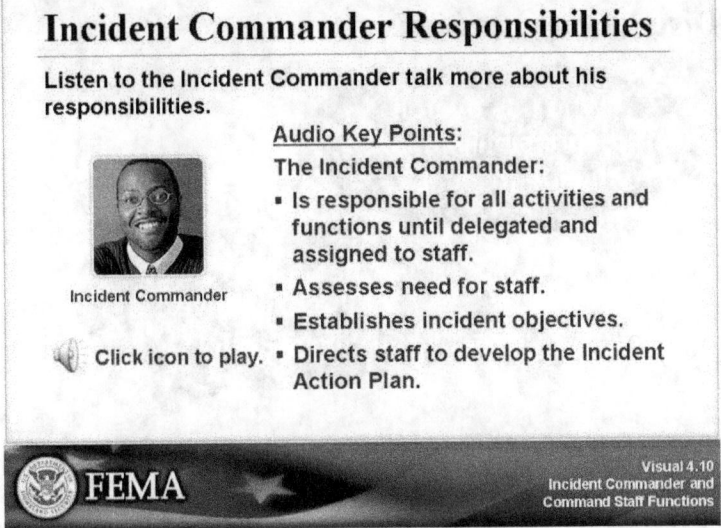

Visual Description: Incident Commander Responsibilities

Instructor Notes

Tell the group that they will now listen to an audio clip in which an Incident Commander talks about his responsibilities.

To play the audio, click on the icon. The total running time for this clip is 41 seconds.

Audio Transcript:

As the Incident Commander, I am responsible for all activities and functions until I delegate them. So, one of the first things I do is assess my need for staff. I know that for an incident that is both complex and long term, I will need more staff. In addition, I may decide that I need a Deputy.

Also, I establish incident objectives for the organization based on the situation and direction given by the campus administration. The type of plan depends on the magnitude of the incident. Most simple incidents don't require written plans. If it were a complex incident, I would direct my staff to develop a written Incident Action Plan. The benefit of ICS is that the organization can be tailored to match the need.

Topic | **Incident Commander**

Visual 4.11

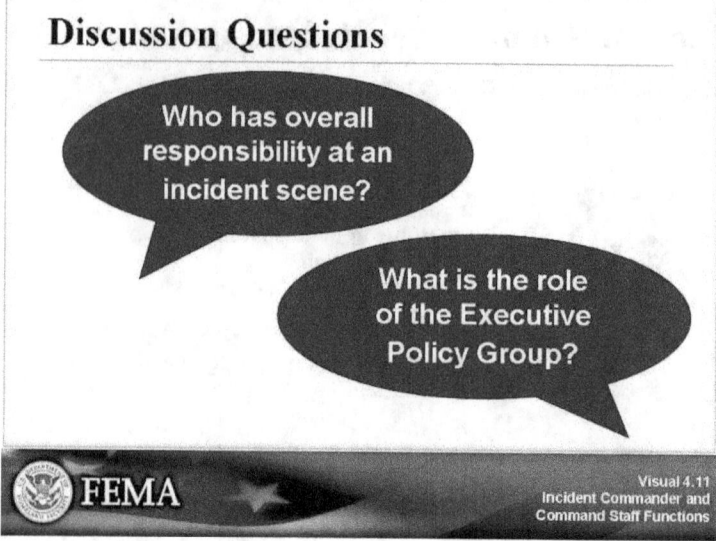

Visual Description: Discussion Questions: Who has overall responsibility at an incident scene? What is the role of the Executive Policy Group?

Instructor Notes

Ask the following questions:

Who has overall responsibility at an incident scene?

Allow time to respond.

If not mentioned, tell the participants that the correct answer is that the Incident Commander has overall responsibility at an incident scene.

What is the role of the Executive Policy Group?

Allow time to respond.

If not mentioned, explain that the Executive Policy Group provides the following to the Incident Commander:
- Policy
- Mission
- Direction
- Authority

| Topic | Deputy Incident Commander |

Visual 4.12

Deputy Incident Commander

A Deputy Incident Commander may be designated to:

- Perform specific tasks as requested by the Incident Commander.
- Perform the incident command function in a relief capacity.
- Represent an assisting agency that shares jurisdiction.

FEMA

Visual 4.12
Incident Commander and
Command Staff Functions

Visual Description: Deputy Incident Commander

Instructor Notes

Tell the group that a Deputy Incident Commander may be designated to:

- Perform specific tasks as requested by the Incident Commander.
- Perform the incident command function in a relief capacity.
- Represent an assisting agency that shares jurisdiction.

Note that if a Deputy is assigned, he or she must be fully qualified to assume the Incident Commander's position.

| Topic | Deputy Incident Commander |

Visual 4.13

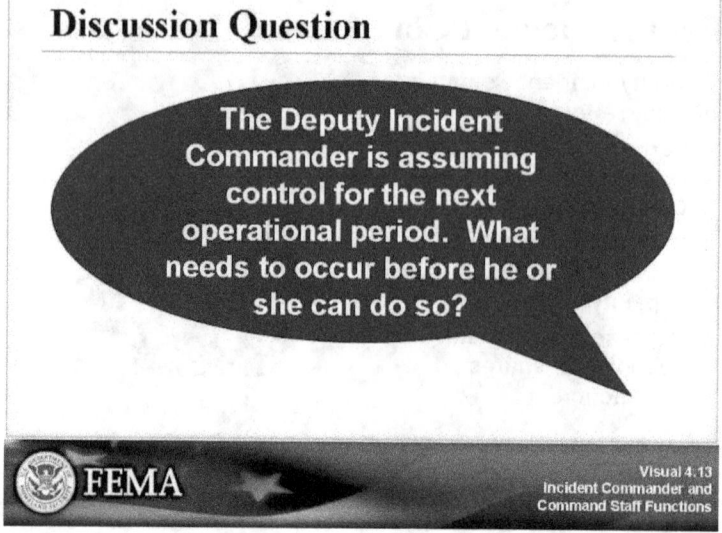

Visual Description: Discussion Question: The Deputy Incident Commander is assuming control for the next operational period. What needs to occur before he or she can do so?

Instructor Notes

Ask the following question:

The Deputy Incident Commander is assuming control for the next operational period. What needs to occur before he or she can do so?

Allow time to respond.

If not mentioned, tell the participants that the correct answer is that before the Deputy Incident Commander can assume control for the next operational period, there must be a transfer of command briefing and notification to all personnel that a change in command is taking place.

Visual 4.14

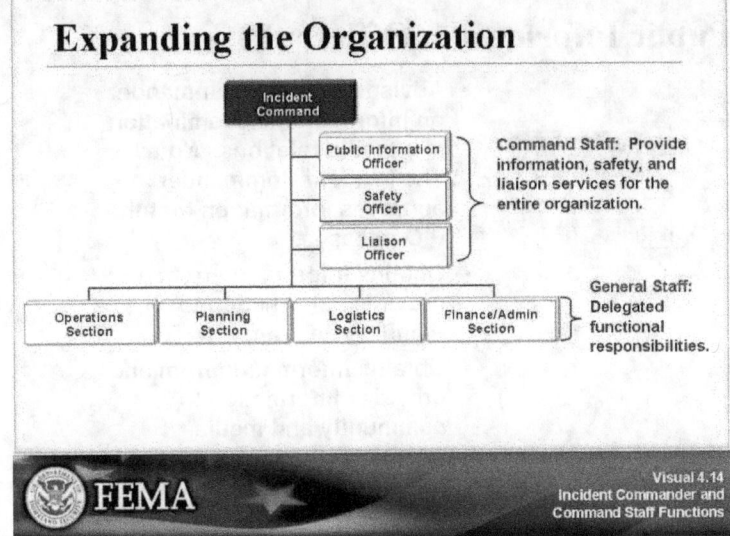

Visual Description: Expanding the Organization

Instructor Notes

As incidents grow, the Incident Commander may delegate authority for performance of certain activities to the Command Staff and the General Staff.

The Incident Commander will add positions only as needed.

Visual 4.15

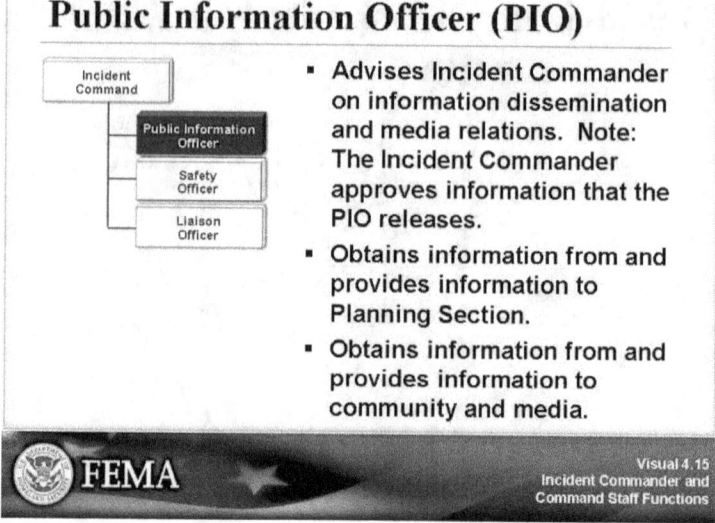

Visual Description: Public Information Officer (PIO)

Instructor Notes

Explain to the participants that the Public Information Officer (PIO):

- Advises the Incident Commander on information dissemination and media relations. Note that the Incident Commander approves information that the PIO releases.
- Obtains information from and provides information to the Planning Section.
- Obtains information from and provides information to the community and media.

| Topic | Command Staff |

Visual 4.16

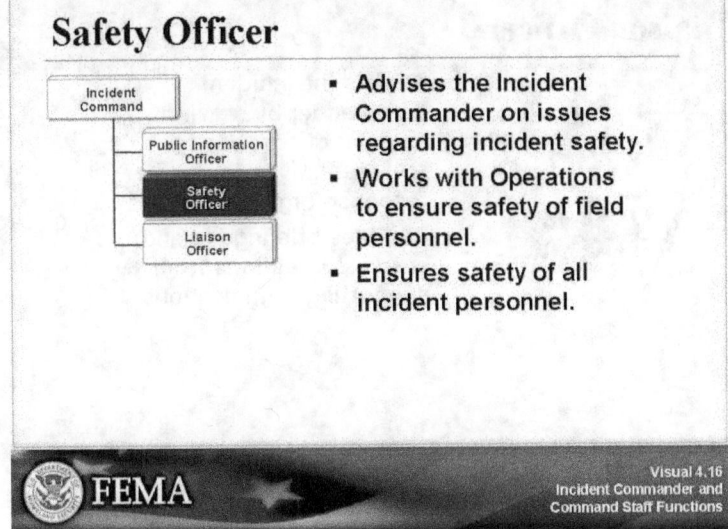

Visual Description: Safety Officer

Instructor Notes

Explain to the participants that the Safety Officer:

- Advises the Incident Commander on issues regarding incident safety.
- Works with the Operations Section to ensure safety of field personnel.
- Ensures the safety of all incident personnel.

Visual 4.17

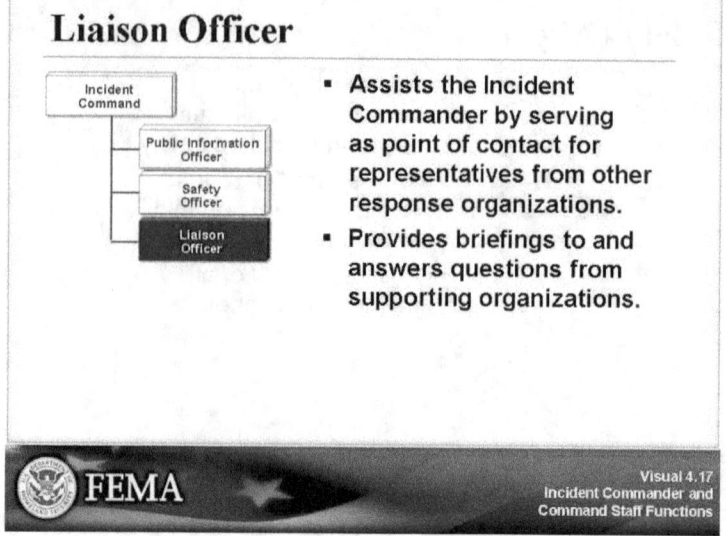

Visual Description: Liaison Officer

Instructor Notes

Explain to the participants that the Liaison Officer:

- Assists the Incident Commander by serving as a point of contact for representatives from other response organizations.
- Provides briefings to and answer questions from supporting organizations.

| Topic | Command Staff |

Visual 4.18

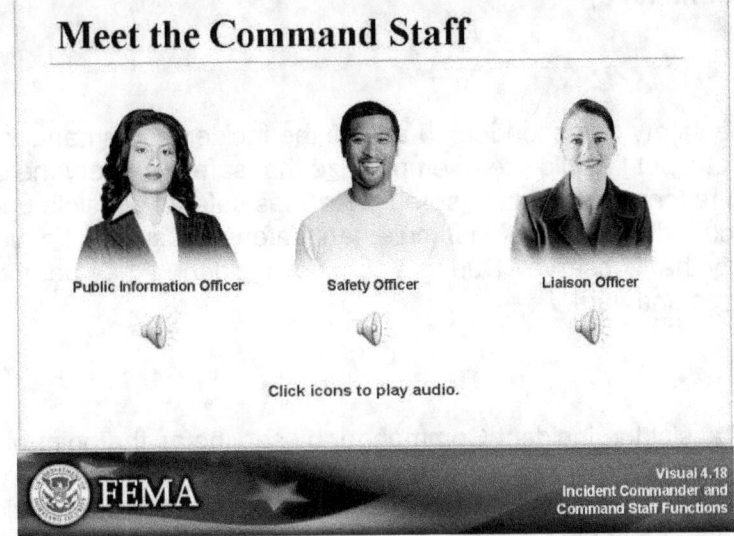

Visual Description: Meet the Command Staff

Instructor Notes

Tell the participants they will hear the Public Information Officer, Safety Officer, and Liaison Officer explain their roles as part of the Command Staff.

Click on each position to hear the audio transcript.

Audio Transcript:

Public Information Officer

I report directly to the Incident Commander. I am the primary contact for anyone who wants information about the incident and our response to it. I provide information to the media, public, and the campus community. Campus incidents attract a lot of media attention. Without me, media requests would overwhelm the Incident Commander. I also coordinate communications to our internal audiences including both incident staff and campus personnel. It's very important for me to coordinate with other public information staff in the policy group to ensure that we do not issue confusing or conflicting information.

Accurate information is essential. In the end, the Incident Commander will approve all information released at the scene. Other information may be released by the Executive Policy Group. During a complex incident, I may need an assistant to help me.

Audio Transcript: (Continued)

Safety Officer

My job is to ensure the safety of responders. I advise the Incident Commander on issues regarding incident safety, but I would like to emphasize that safety is everyone's responsibility. I work very closely with responders to make sure they are as safe as possible under the circumstances. I conduct risk analyses and implement safety measures. I have the authority to stop any unsafe activity that I observe. During a complex incident, I may need quite a few assistants to be my eyes and ears.

Liaison Officer

I'm the go-between. I assist the Incident Commander by serving as the point of contact for other response organizations providing resources at the scene. I facilitate coordination with the Executive Policy Group, adjacent jurisdictions, and nongovernmental organizations. I respond to requests from incident personnel for contacts among the assisting and cooperating agencies. I also monitor incident operations in order to identify any current or potential problems between the institution and response agencies.

| Topic | Command Staff |

Visual 4.19

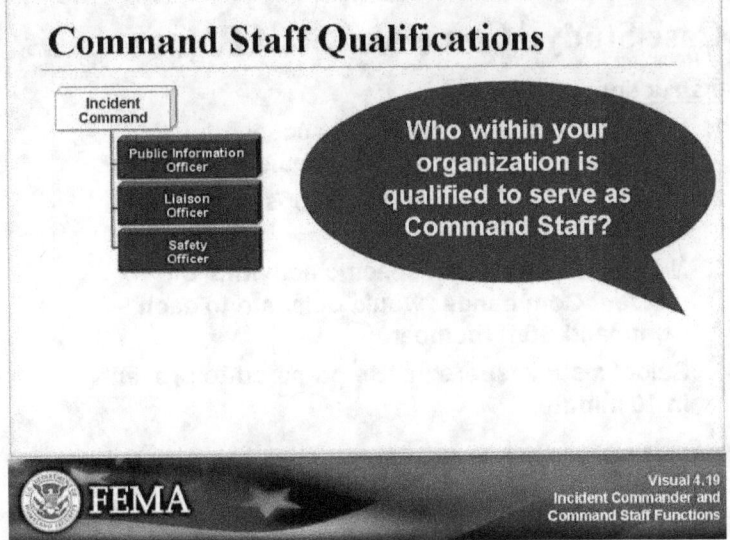

Visual Description: Command Staff Qualifications: Who within your organization is qualified to serve as Command Staff?

Instructor Notes

Depending upon the size and type of incident or event, the Incident Commander may designate personnel to provide information, safety, and liaison services. In ICS, the following personnel comprise the Command Staff:

- Public Information Officer, who serves as the conduit for information to internal and external stakeholders, including the media or parents.

- Safety Officer, who monitors safety conditions and develops measures for assuring the safety of all response personnel.

- Liaison Officer, who serves as the primary contact for supporting agencies assisting at an incident.

Ask the participants: Who within your organization is qualified to serve as Command Staff?

| Topic | Case Study: Command Staff Roles |

Visual 4.20

Case Study: Command Staff Roles

<u>Instructions</u>:

1. Working as a team, review the case study presented in your Student Manuals.
2. Identify which Command Staff positions would be assigned.
3. Next, determine what specific activities the Incident Commander would delegate to each Command Staff member.
4. Select a spokesperson. Be prepared to present in 10 minutes.

FEMA

Visual 4.20
Incident Commander and
Command Staff Functions

Visual Description: Case Study: Command Staff Roles

Instructor Notes

Purpose: The purpose of this activity is to illustrate how ICS can be used to address incident management issues.

Instructions: Follow the steps below to conduct this activity:

1. Working as a team, review the case study presented on the next page of your Student Manuals.
2. Identify which Command Staff positions would be assigned.
3. Next, if you were the Incident Commander, what specific activities would you delegate to each Command Staff member?
4. Select a spokesperson. Be prepared to present in 10 minutes.

Scenario:

An unexpected flash flood has struck a small community. As a result:

- Homes, schools, the business district, and the community college are being evacuated.
- Critical infrastructure has been damaged including contamination of the water supply, downed power lines, and damaged roads.
- Perimeter control and security in the business district are needed.
- Mutual aid is arriving from several surrounding communities.
- Media representatives are arriving at the scene.

Questions:

1. **Which Command Staff positions would be assigned?**

2. **If you were the Incident Commander, what specific activities would you delegate to each Command Staff member?**

Debrief: Monitor the time. When 10 minutes have passed, ask the spokesperson from each group to present their Command Staff positions assigned and the activities that were delegated. If not mentioned by the group, add the following potential activities:

- **Public Information Officer:** Work with the media to ensure that evacuation orders are communicated to affected neighbors. Prepare releases with information about the status of the business district prior to the next morning. Arrange a press briefing in advance of the next news cycle.
- **Liaison Officer:** Coordinate with communities that are providing mutual aid and with private-sector utilities that are supporting the response. Work with the business community to identify response needs.
- **Safety Officer:** Ensure the safety of incident personnel from contaminated waste water, electrical hazards, and fatigue.

Topic   Summary

Visual 4.21

> ## Summary
>
> Are you now able to:
> - Identify the five major ICS management functions?
> - Identify the position titles associated with the Command Staff?
> - Describe the role and function of the Incident Commander?
> - Describe the role and function of the Command Staff?
>
> **FEMA**
>
> Visual 4.21
> Incident Commander and
> Command Staff Functions

Visual Description: Summary

Instructor Notes

Ask the participants if they are able to:

- Identify the five major ICS management functions.
- Identify the position titles associated with the Command Staff.
- Describe the role and function of the Incident Commander.
- Describe the role and function of the Command Staff.

Answer any questions the participants might have about this unit.

Explain that the next unit will discuss the roles and responsibilities of the General Staff.

Unit 5: General Staff Functions

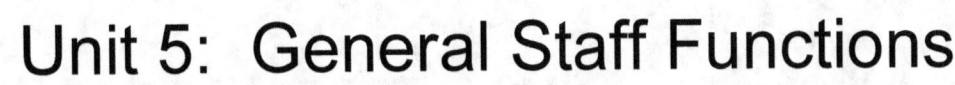

Objective

At the end of this unit, the participants should be able to describe the roles and functions of the General Staff, including:

- Operations Section.
- Planning Section.
- Logistics Section.
- Finance/Administration Section.

Scope

- Unit Introduction
- Unit Objective
- General Staff Overview
  - Expanding Incidents
  - ICS Supervisory Position Titles
  - Activity: ICS Section Chiefs and Deputies
  - Increasing Interagency Coordination
- Operations Section
  - Operations Section: Major Activities
  - Audio: Operations Section Chief
  - Video: Operations Section: Expanding and Contracting
  - Operations: Single Resources
  - Operations: Teams
  - Sample Strike Teams and Task Forces
  - Activity
  - Operations: Too Many Teams!
  - The Solution: Add Functional Groups
  - Geographic Divisions & Groups
  - Complex Incidents
  - Activity: What Is the Correct Title?
- Planning Section
  - Planning Section: Major Activities
  - Audio: Planning Section Chief
  - Planning Section: Units
  - Knowledge Review
- Logistics Section
  - Logistics Section: Major Activities
  - Audio: Logistics Section Chief
  - Logistics Section: Branches and Units
- Finance/Administration Section
  - Finance/Administration Section: Major Activities
  - Audio: Finance/Administration Section Chief
  - Finance/Administration Section: Units
- Review Activity: Which Section Chief?
- Case Study: General Staff Functions
- Summary

Methodology

The instructors will outline this unit's objective. They will then explain that as incidents expand, there may be need to add supervisory layers to the organization structure. This unit will describe these layers in depth and, specifically, will explain the role of the General Staff in the ICS structure.

The instructors will then explain the importance of using specific ICS position titles. They will identify the titles for all ICS supervisory levels.

The instructors will start with the Operations Section, having the participants listen to an audio clip of an Operations Section Chief describing her role. The participants will then watch a video describing how the Operations Section may expand or contract. The instructors will further explain the role of Task Forces, Strike Teams, and Single Resources. The participants will complete an activity applying ICS position titles within an expanding Operations Section.

To introduce the Planning Section, the instructors will present an audio clip of a Planning Section Chief describing his job. The instructors will then overview the key Planning Section tasks, and discuss the roles of the four Planning Section Units. They will also explain the use of Technical Specialists. The participants will complete a Knowledge Review matching particular Planning Section Units to specific functions.

The instructors will then identify the tasks of the Logistics Section. The participants will listen to an audio clip of the Logistics Section Chief describing his role. The instructors will then describe the Service Branch and the Support Branch and their corresponding Units.

The instructors will then present an audio clip of a Finance/Administration Section Chief describing her role. The instructors will then outline the major tasks of the Finance/Administration Section. The instructors will then describe each of the four Finance/Administration Section Units.

The participants will then complete an activity that allows them to apply the information they have learned about General Staff roles and responsibilities.

To summarize the unit, the instructors will present a case study scenario in which the participants must answer questions that assess their understanding of the role of the General Staff. After discussing the questions based on the scenario, the instructors will ask the participants if they have met the learning objective for this unit.

Time Plan

A suggested time plan for this unit is shown below. More or less time may be required, based on the experience level of the group.

Topic	Time
Unit Introduction and Unit Objectives	5 minutes
General Staff	10 minutes
Operations Section	15 minutes
Activities	20 minutes
Planning Section	10 minutes
Logistics Section	10 minutes
Finance/Administration Section	10 minutes
Activity	5 minutes
Case Study: General Staff Functions	15 minutes
Summary	5 minutes
Total Time	**1 hour 45 minutes**

This page intentionally left blank.

| Topic | Unit Introduction |

Visual 5.1

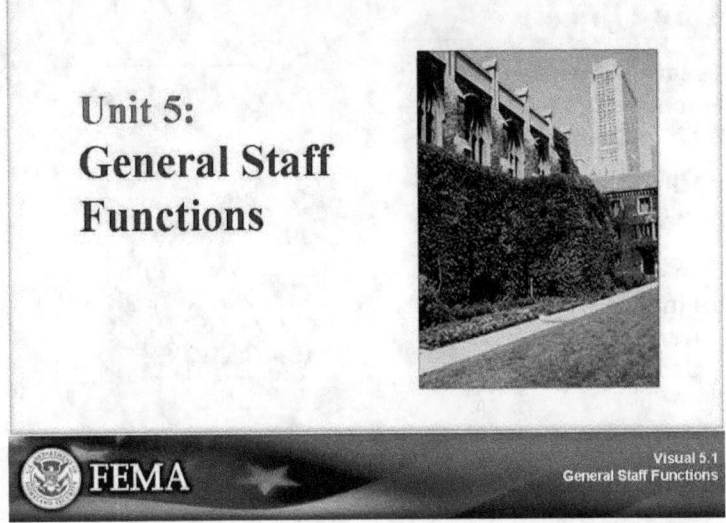

Visual Description: Unit Introduction

Instructor Notes

Tell the participants that this unit will provide an overview of ICS General Staff functions, including the following topics:

- Operations Section
- Planning Section
- Logistics Section
- Finance/Administration Section

The unit concludes with a case study exercise in which the students will apply what they have learned about the General Staff.

| Topic | Unit Objective |

Visual 5.2

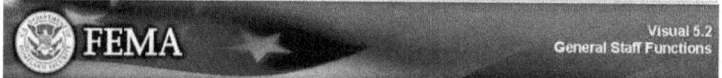

Unit Objective

Describe the roles and functions of the General Staff including:

- Operations Section
- Planning Section
- Logistics Section
- Finance/ Administration Section

FEMA

Visual 5.2
General Staff Functions

Visual Description: Unit Objective

Instructor Notes

Tell participants that by the end of this unit, they should be able to describe the roles and functions of the General Staff including:

- Operations Section
- Planning Section
- Logistics Section
- Finance/Administration Section

Remind the participants that most incidents usually are small, managed in a short period of time, and require few outside response resources. However, an institution may become involved in a larger incident affecting the whole community and may be isolated. In such cases, a larger ICS organization may be required to manage the incident.

Topic	General Staff

Visual 5.3

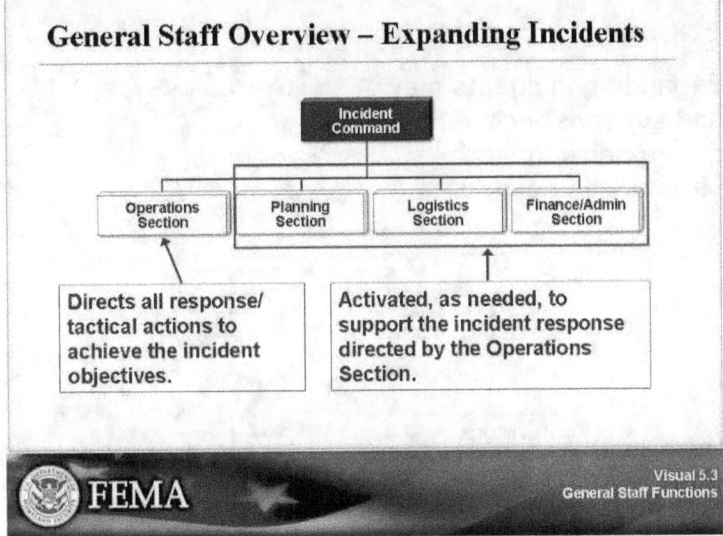

Visual Description: General Staff Overview – Expanding Incidents

Instructor Notes

Tell participants that the General Staff overall responsibilities are summarized in the graphic.

In an expanding incident, the Incident Command first establishes the Operations Section. The remaining Sections are established as needed to support the operation.

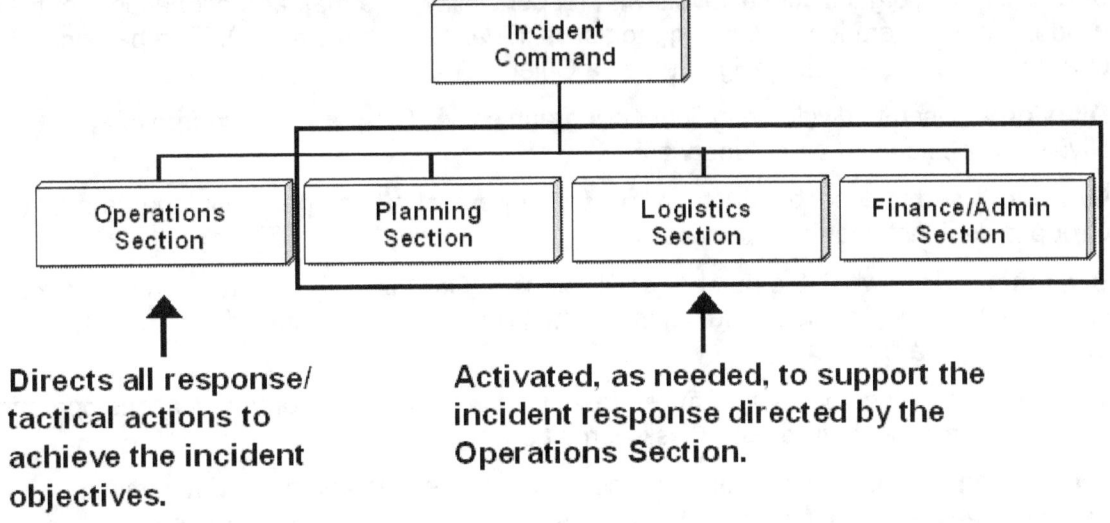

Visual 5.4

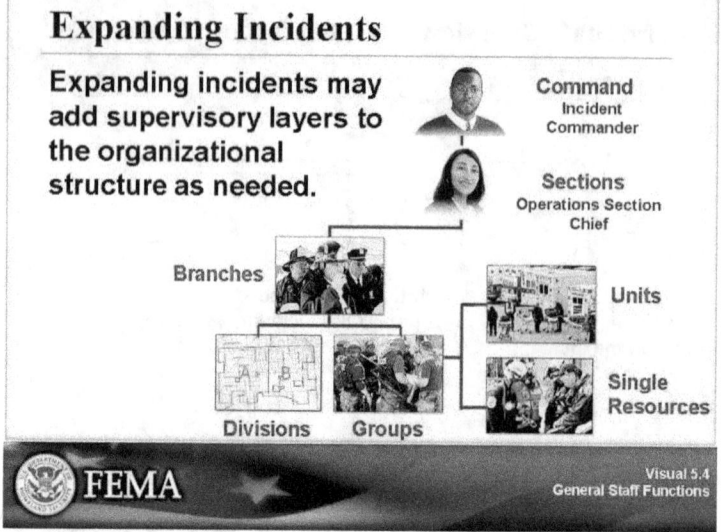

Visual Description: Expanding Incidents

Instructor Notes

Tell the participants that the definitions of ICS organizational components are shown in the Student Manual.

Note that later they will learn more about the different organizational elements.

- **Sections:** The organizational levels with responsibility for a major functional area of the incident (e.g., Operations, Planning, Logistics, Finance/Administration). The person in charge of each Section is designated as a Chief.

- **Divisions:** Used to divide an incident geographically. The person in charge of each Division is designated as a Supervisor.

- **Groups:** Used to describe functional areas of operations. The person in charge of each Group is designated as a Supervisor.

- **Branches:** Used when the number of Divisions or Groups exceeds the span of control. Can be either geographical or functional. The person in charge of each Branch is designated as a Director.

- **Task Forces:** A combination of mixed resources with common communications operating under the direct supervision of a Task Force Leader.

- **Strike Teams:** A set number of resources of the same kind and type with common communications operating under the direct supervision of a Strike Team Leader.

- **Single Resources:** May be individuals, a piece of equipment and its personnel complement, or a crew or team of individuals with an identified supervisor that can be used at an incident.

| Topic | General Staff |

Visual 5.5

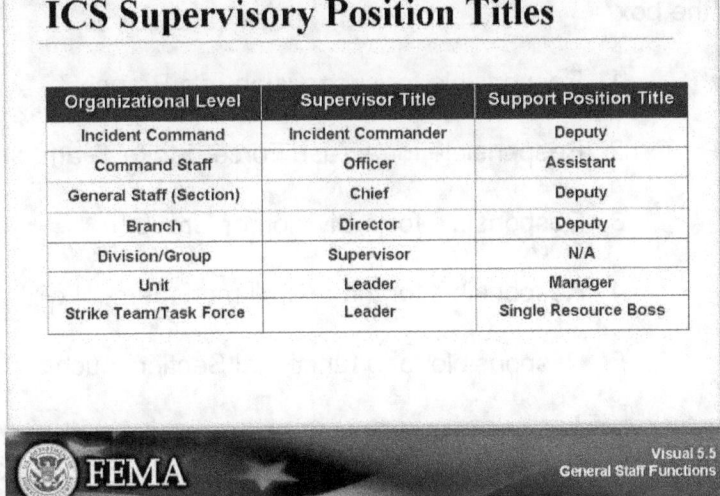

Visual Description: ICS Supervisory Position Titles

Instructor Notes

Tell the participants that additional levels of supervision are added as the ICS organization expands.

The ICS supervisory titles are shown in the graphic.

Organizational Level	Supervisor Title	Support Position Title
Incident Command	Incident Commander	Deputy
Command Staff	Officer	Assistant
General Staff (Section)	Chief	Deputy
Branch	Director	Deputy
Division/Group	Supervisor	N/A
Unit	Leader	Manager
Strike Team/Task Force	Leader	Single Resource Boss

Topic   Activity

Instructions: Match the title below with the correct description by placing the correct description number in the box.

☐	Commander	1.	Responsible for supervision of a Branch.
☐	Chief	2.	Responsible for a Task Force, Strike Team, or functional Unit.
☐	Director	3.	Responsible for a Division or Group.
☐	Supervisor	4.	Responsible for the overall management of the incident.
☐	Leader	5.	Responsible for a functional Section, such as Operations.

Allow the participants 2 minutes to mark their responses in their Student Manuals.

Review the correct answers as shown below:

4	The **Incident Commander** is responsible for the overall management of the incident.
5	A **Section Chief** is responsible for a functional Section, such as Operations.
1	A **Branch Director** is responsible for supervision of a Branch.
3	A **Supervisor** is responsible for a Division or Group.
2	A **Leader** is responsible for a Task Force, Strike Team, or functional Unit.

Topic	General Staff

Visual 5.6

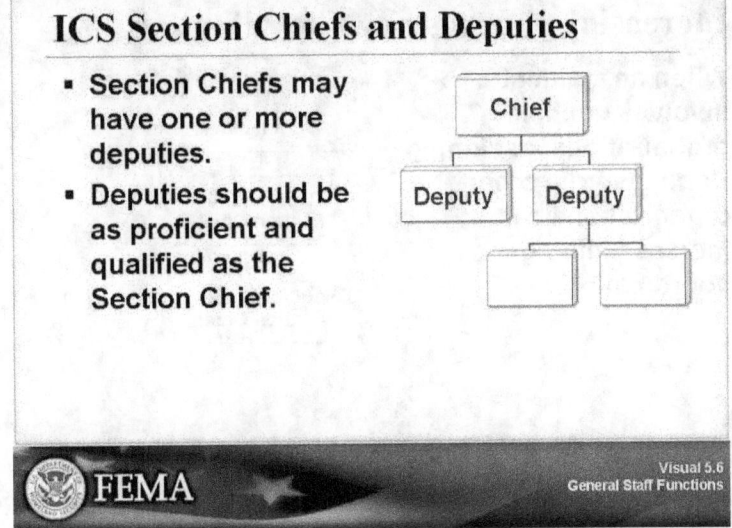

Visual Description: ICS Section Chiefs and Deputies

Instructor Notes

Tell the participants that, as mentioned previously, the person in charge of each Section is designated as a Chief. Section Chiefs have the ability to expand their Sections to meet the needs of the situation.

Each of the Section Chiefs may have a Deputy, or more than one, if necessary. The Deputy:

- May assume responsibility for a specific portion of the primary position, work as relief, or be assigned other tasks.

- Should always be as proficient as the person for whom he or she works.

Topic	General Staff

Visual 5.7

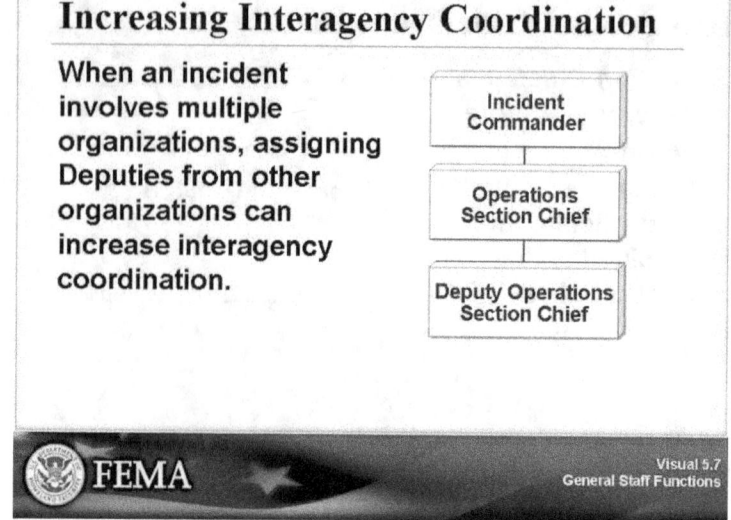

Visual Description: Increasing Interagency Coordination

Instructor Notes

Explain that when an incident involves multiple organizations, assigning Deputies from other organizations can increase interagency coordination.

For example, in the case of a bomb threat on campus, command may be transferred to a first response organization while a campus public safety officer may serve as a Deputy. When first responders and campus personnel are integrated into the same ICS organizational structure, valuable information can be shared and crisis decisionmaking improved.

Topic	Operations Section

Visual 5.8

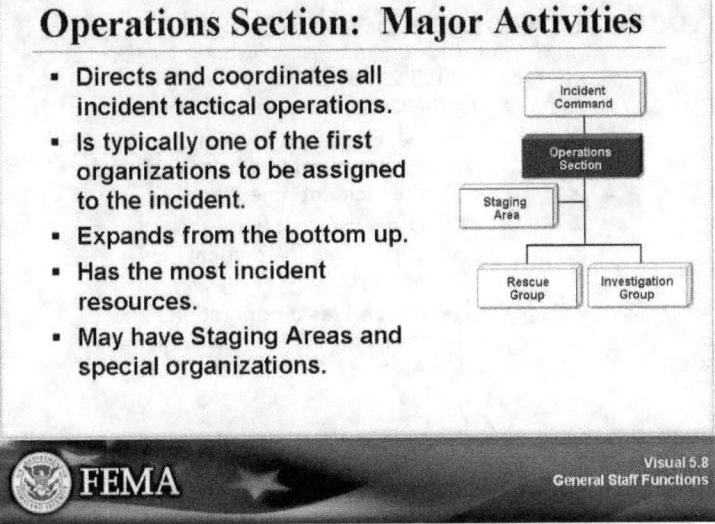

Visual Description: Operations Section: Major Activities

Instructor Notes

Explain that the Operations Section is responsible for directing and coordinating all incident tactical operations.

Review the following key points with the group:

The Operations Section:

- Is typically one of the first organizations to be assigned to the incident.
- Develops from the bottom up.
- Has the most incident resources.
- May have Staging Areas and special organizations.

Topic	Operations Section

Visual 5.9

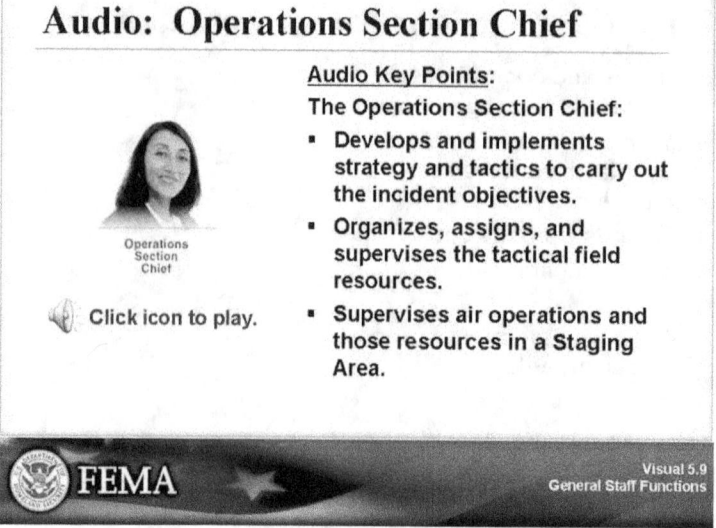

Visual Description: Audio: Operations Section Chief

Instructor Notes

Present the following points to the participants:

Typically, the Operations Section Chief is the person with the greatest technical and tactical expertise in dealing with the problem at hand. The Operations Section Chief:

- Develops and implements strategy and tactics to carry out the incident objectives.
- Organizes, assigns, and supervises the response resources.

Tell the participants that they will listen to an audio clip of an Operations Section Chief explaining her role.

Audio Transcript:

I take direction from the Incident Commander. I'm responsible for developing and implementing strategy and tactics to accomplish the incident objectives. This means that I organize, assign, and supervise all the tactical or response resources assigned to the incident. I would also manage the Staging Area, if one were established.

Topic	Video: Operations Section: Expanding and Contracting

Visual 5.10

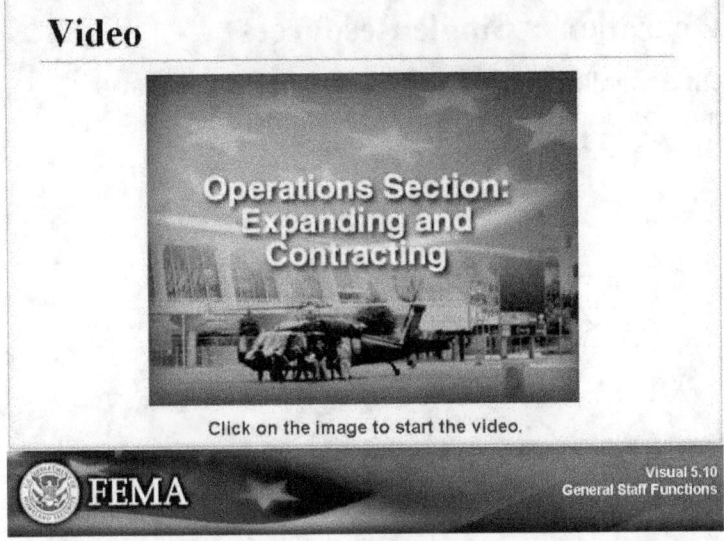

Visual Description: Video: Operations Section: Expanding and Contracting

---

Instructor Notes

Tell the participants that you are going to play a short video that explains how the Section Chief manages the Operations Section. The video summarizes the expansion and contraction of an Operations Section.

Video Transcript:

The Operations Section Chief at an incident may work initially with only a few single resources or staff members.

The Operations Section usually develops from the bottom up. The organization will expand to include needed levels of supervision as more and more resources are deployed.

Single resources may be grouped into Strike Teams or Task Forces who report to a Leader. Remember, Strike Teams are comprised of similar resources while Task Forces combine different types of resources.

Groups may be added to supervise the growing number of resources, Teams, or Task Forces. Or, geographic Divisions along with Groups may be used. The Operations Section Chief may add Branches to supervise the Groups and Divisions and further reduce his or her span of control.

At some point, the Operations Section and the rest of the ICS organization will contract. The decision to contract will be based on the achievement of incident objectives.

Demobilization planning begins upon activation of the first personnel and continues until the ICS organization ceases operation.

| Topic | Operations Section |

Visual 5.11

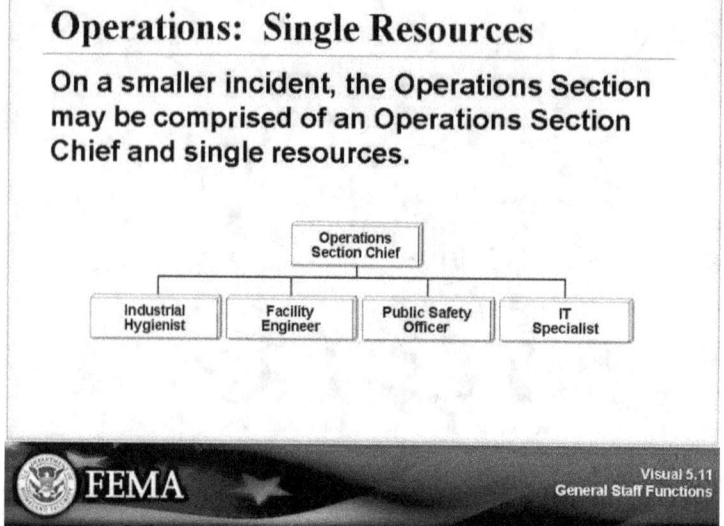

Visual Description: Operations: Single Resources

Instructor Notes

Present the following points:

Single Resources are individuals, a piece of equipment and its personnel complement, or a crew or team of individuals with an identified supervisor. On a smaller incident, the Operations Section may be comprised of an Operations Section Chief and single resources.

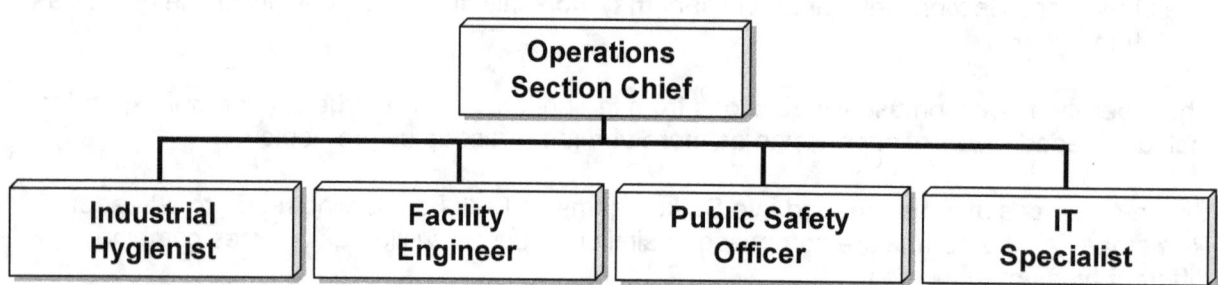

Topic	Operations Section

Visual 5.12

Operations: Teams

Single resources may be organized into teams. Using standard ICS terminology, the two types of team configurations are:

- Task Forces, which are a <u>combination of mixed resources</u> with common communications supervised by a Leader.
- Strike Teams, which include all <u>similar resources</u> with common communications supervised by a Leader.

FEMA

Visual 5.12
General Staff Functions

Visual Description: Operations: Teams

Instructor Notes

Summarize the following key points:

Single resources may be organized into teams. Using standard ICS terminology, the two types of team configurations are:

- **Task Forces,** which are a combination of **<u>mixed resources</u>** with common communications operating under the direct supervision of a Leader.

- **Strike Teams,** which include all **<u>similar resources</u>** with common communications operating under the direct supervision of a Leader.

Topic | **Operations Section**

Visual 5.13

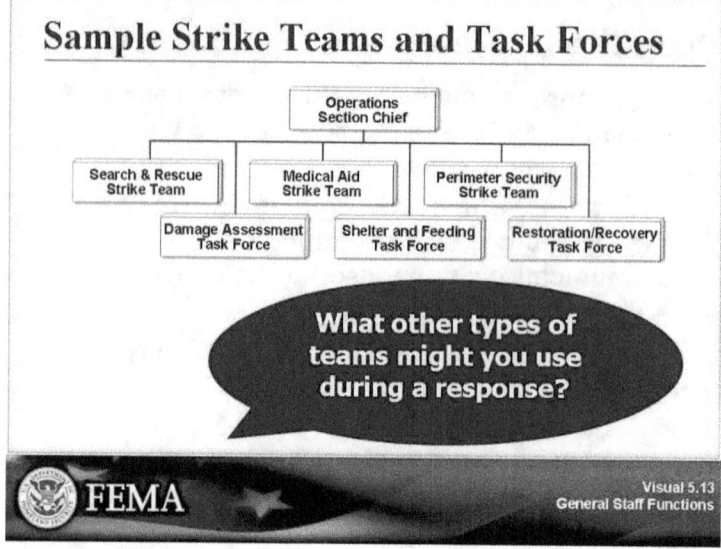

Visual Description: Sample Strike Teams and Task Forces

Instructor Notes

Point out that the Operations Section organization chart shows possible team assignments in a campus incident. Each team would have a Team Leader reporting to the Operations Section Chief.

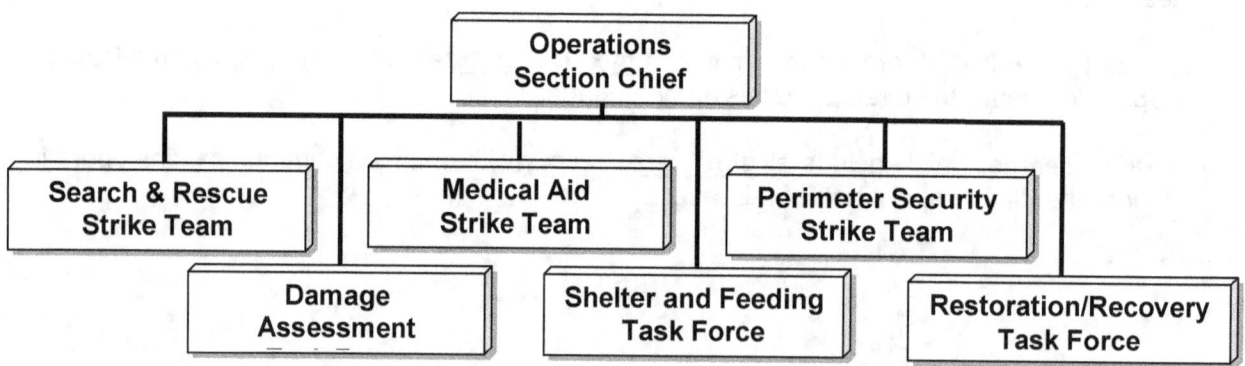

Note that these are examples of possible teams. Teams should be established based on the type of incident and unique requirements of the campus.

Ask the participants: What other types of teams might you use during a response?

| Topic | Operations Section |

Visual 5.14

Visual Description: Activity

Instructor Notes

Review the following scenario: Heavy rains have caused flash flooding. Your campus is isolated and students and staff cannot leave. Help may not arrive for several hours.

Next, ask the participants to work in table groups to complete the following steps:

- Develop an organizational chart depicting how the Operations Section could be organized into teams. Draw the team structure on chart paper as large as possible.

- List the responsibilities of each team.

- Be prepared to present in 15 minutes.

Instructor Note: There is no single correct answer. Have the teams hang up their charts on one wall. Compare the similarities and differences among the team structures.

| Topic | Operations Section |

Visual 5.15

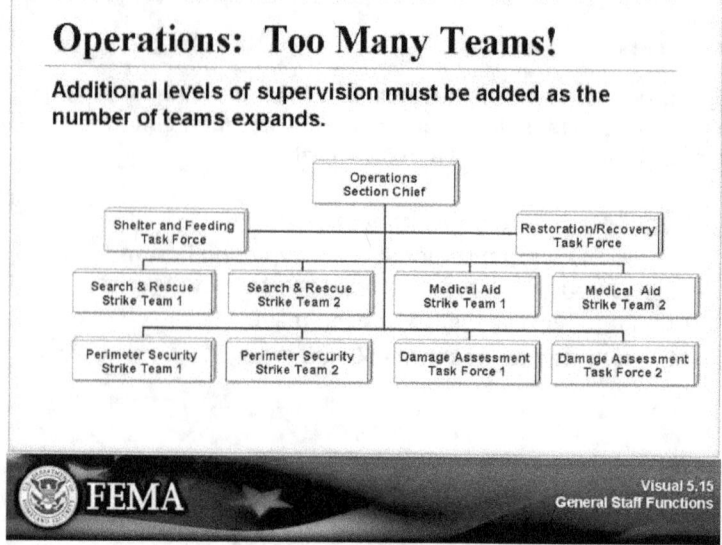

Visual Description: Operations: Too Many Teams!

Instructor Notes

Explain to the participants that, to maintain span of control, each team should be comprised of a Team Leader and no more than 5 to 7 team members.

Ask the participants: As teams are added, what happens to the Operations Section Chief's span of control?

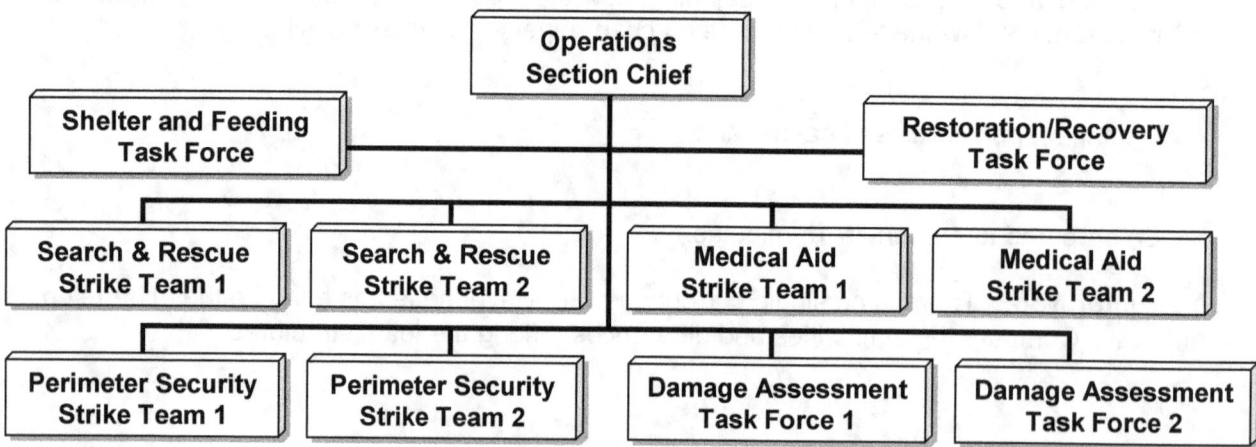

Visual 5.16

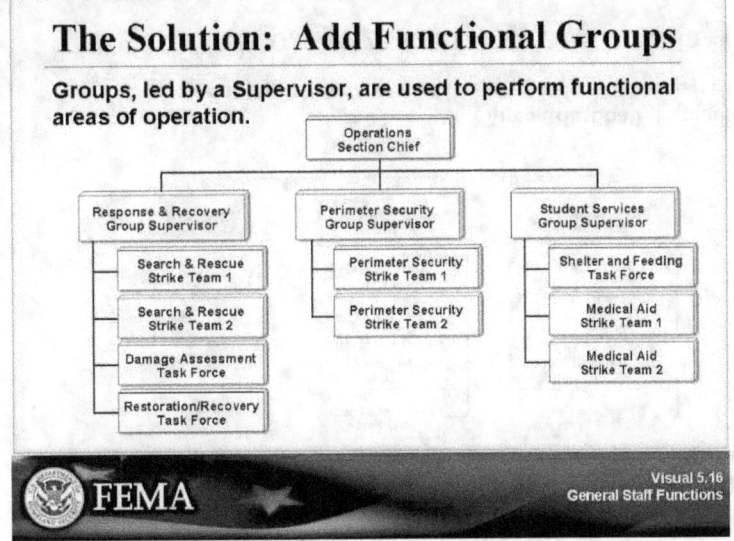

Visual Description: The Solution: Add Functional Groups

Instructor Notes

Point out that, on a large, complex incident the Operations Section may become very large. Using the ICS principle of modular organization, the Operations Section may add elements to manage span of control. **Groups are used to perform functional areas of operation.** The organizational chart below illustrates how Groups can be used to maintain span of control within the Operations Section.

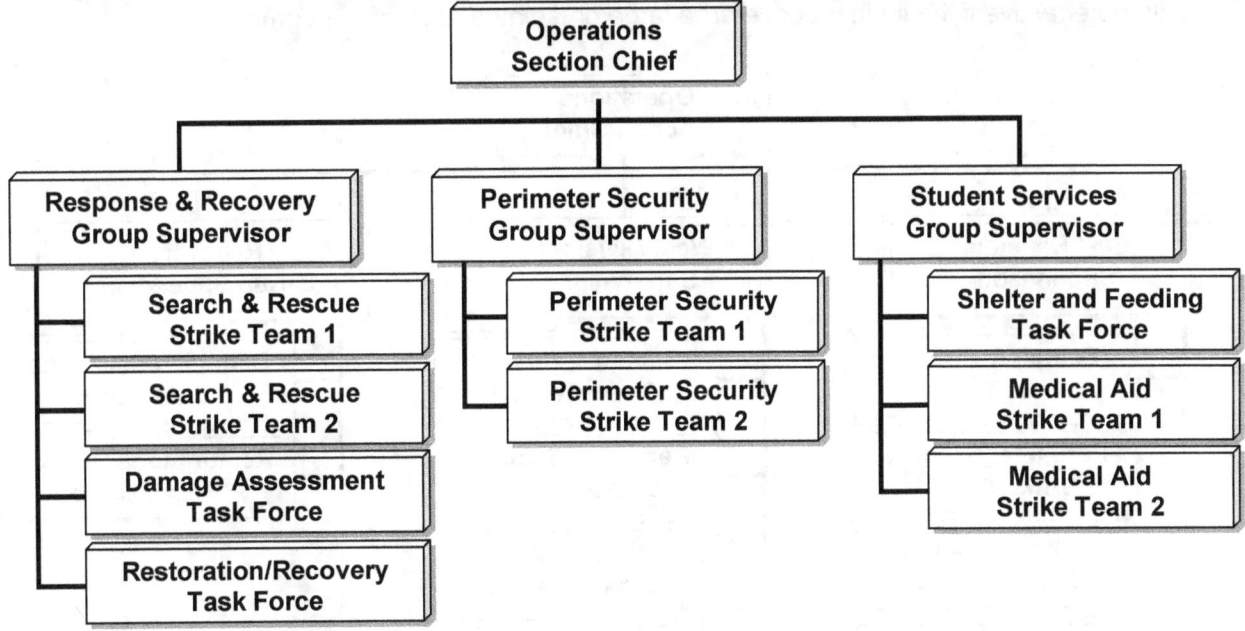

Visual 5.17

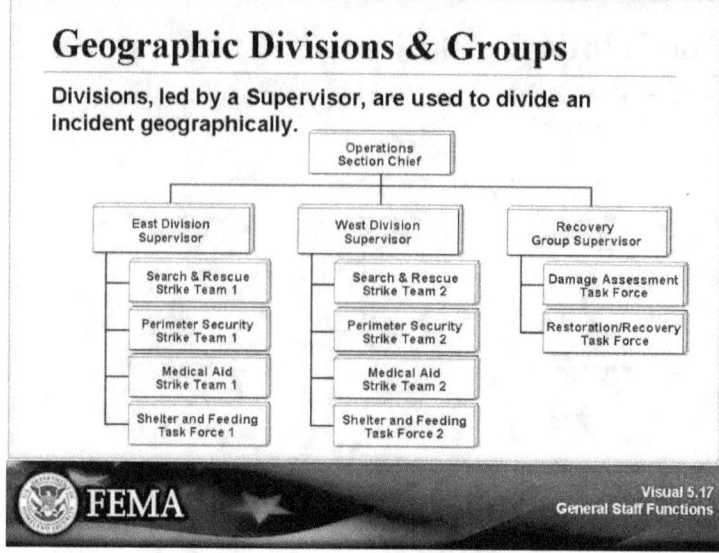

Visual Description: Geographic Divisions & Groups

Instructor Notes

Summarize the following key points:

Divisions can be used to add a level of supervision. Divisions are used to divide an incident geographically. The organizational chart below illustrates how Groups and Divisions can be used together to maintain span of control within the Operations Section. The use of Divisions would be effective if the incident covered a large or isolated area of the campus.

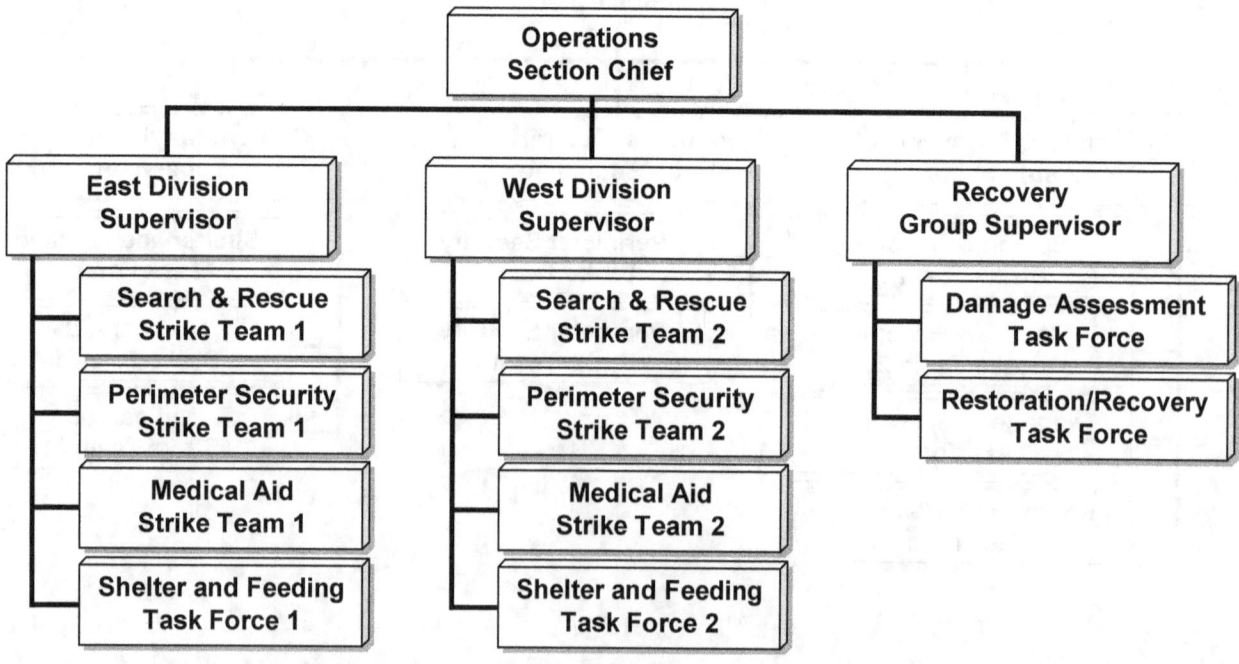

Visual 5.18

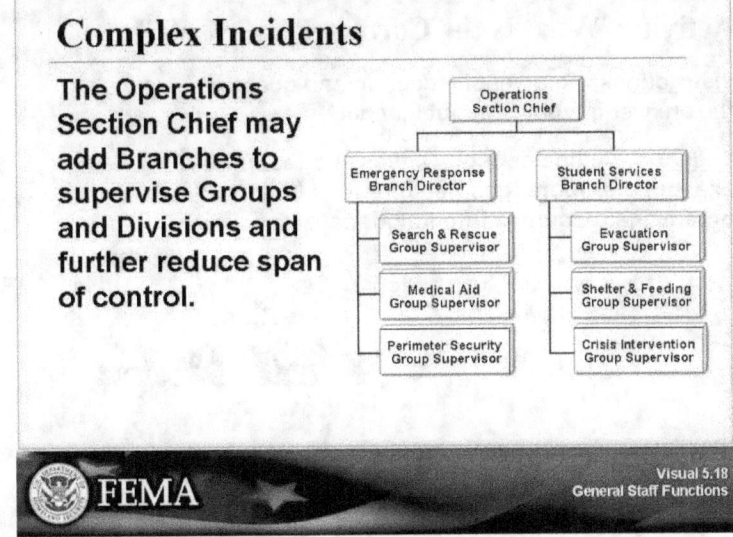

Visual Description: Complex Incidents

Instructor Notes

The Operations Section Chief may add Branches to supervise Groups and Divisions and further reduce his or her span of control. The person in charge of each Branch is designated as a Director.

Review the chart. Ask the participants: What are the advantages of reducing the Operations Section Chief's span of control?

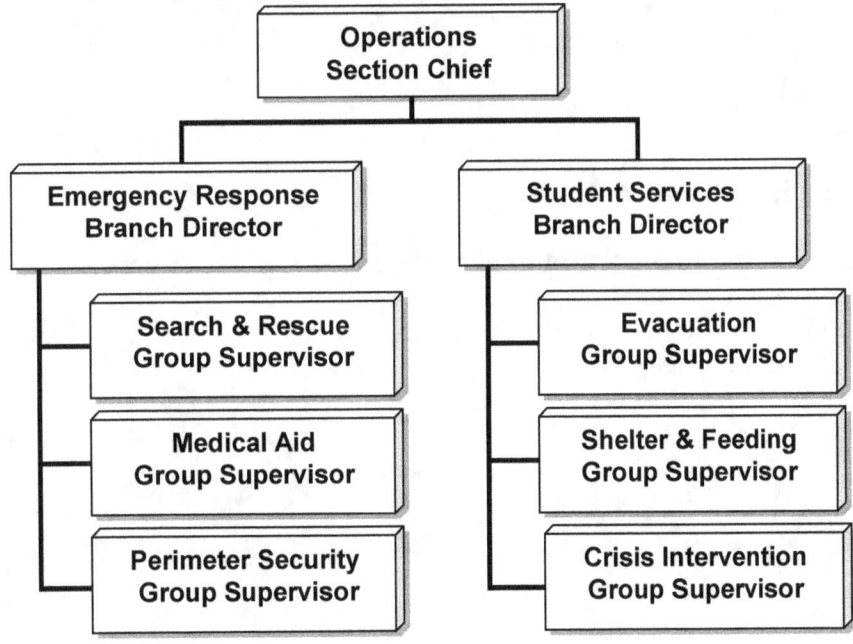

Topic	Operations Section

Visual 5.19

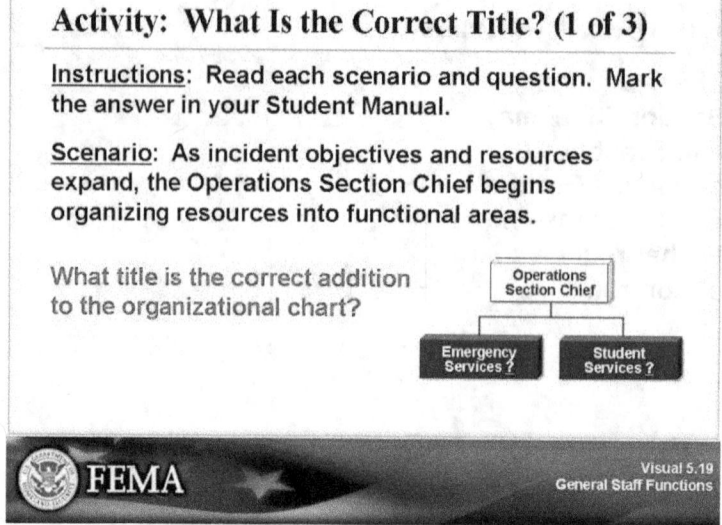

Visual Description: Activity: What Is the Correct Title? (1 of 3)

Instructor Notes

Instructions: Read each scenario and question. Mark the answers in your Student Manual.

Scenario: As incident objectives and resources expand, the Operations Section Chief begins organizing resources into functional areas. What title is the correct addition to the organizational chart?

☐ Unit Supervisor

☐ Team Supervisor

☐ Group Supervisor

Provide feedback on the question:

The correct addition to the organizational chart is: Group Supervisor.

Groups are used to describe functional areas of operations. The person in charge of each Group is designated as a Supervisor.

| Topic | Operations Section |

Visual 5.20

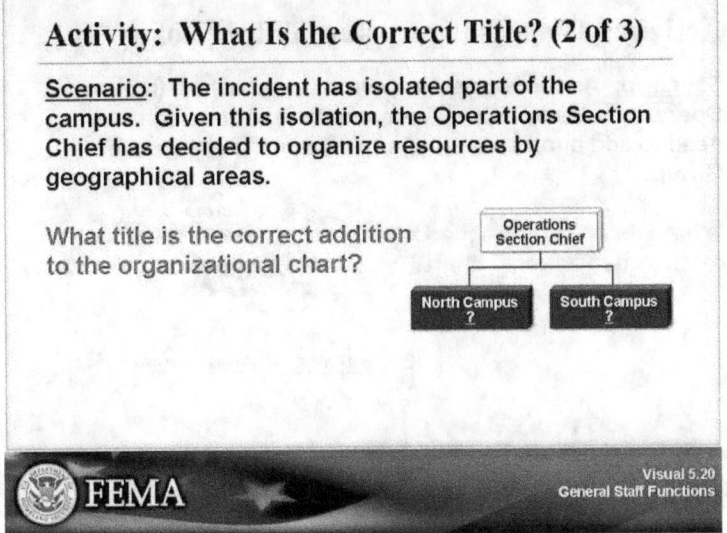

Visual Description: Activity: What Is the Correct Title? (2 of 3)

Instructor Notes

Scenario: The incident has isolated part of the campus. Given this isolation, the Operations Section Chief has decided to organize resources by geographical areas. What title is the correct addition to the organizational chart?

☐ Task Force Supervisor

☐ Division Supervisor

☐ Sector Supervisor

Provide feedback on the question:

The correct addition to the organizational chart is: Division Supervisor.

Divisions are used to divide an incident geographically. The person in charge of each Division is designated as a Supervisor.

Topic	Operations Section

Visual 5.21

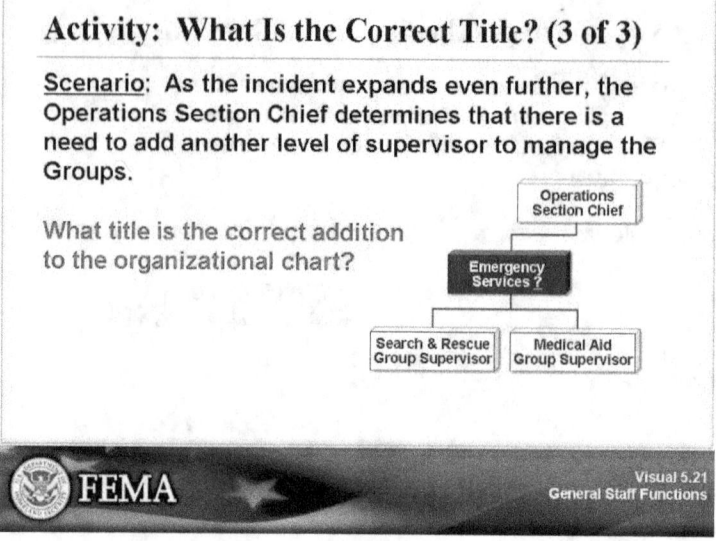

Visual Description: Activity: What Is the Correct Title? (3 of 3)

Instructor Notes

Scenario: As the incident expands even further, the Operations Section Chief determines that there is a need to add another level of supervisor to manage the Groups. What title is the correct addition to the organizational chart?

☐ Branch Director

☐ Department Director

☐ Field Director

Provide feedback on the question:

The correct addition to the organizational chart is: Branch Director.

Branches may be added when the number of Divisions or Groups exceeds the span of control and can be either geographical or functional. The person in charge of each Branch is designated as a Director.

Tell the participants you will look at the Planning Section next.

| Topic | Planning Section |

Visual 5.22

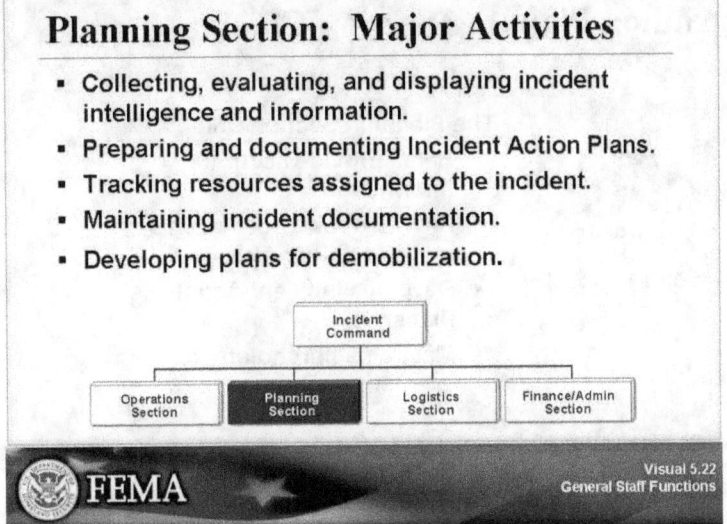

Visual Description: Planning Section: Major Activities

Instructor Notes

Tell the participants that the major activities of the Planning Section may include:

- Collecting, evaluating, and displaying incident intelligence and information.
- Preparing and documenting Incident Action Plans.
- Tracking resources assigned to the incident.
- Maintaining incident documentation.
- Developing plans for demobilization.

Topic	Planning Section

Visual 5.23

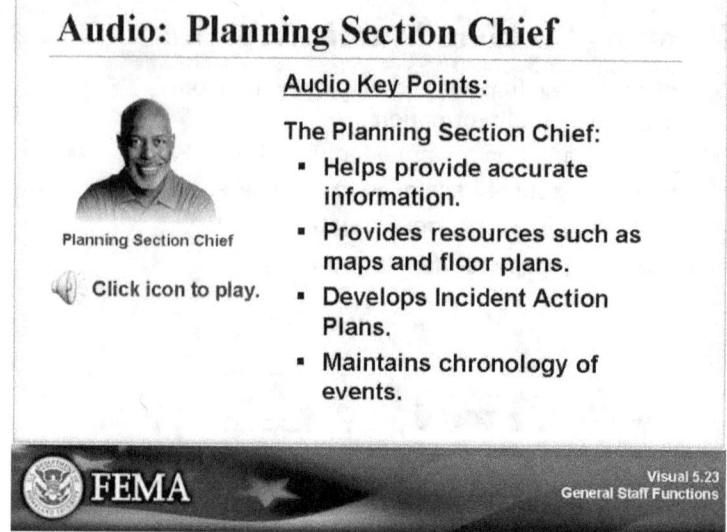

Visual Description: Audio: Planning Section Chief

Instructor Notes

Summarize the following key points:

- The Incident Commander will determine if there is a need for a Planning Section and if so, will designate a Planning Section Chief.

- If no Planning Section is established, the Incident Commander will perform all planning functions.

- It is up to the Planning Section Chief to activate any needed additional staffing.

Tell the participants that you will play a short audio of a Planning Section Chief describing the role of the Planning Section in the ICS organization.

Audio Transcript:

The Incident Commander will determine if there is a need for a Planning Section, and if so, will designate a Planning Section Chief. In a campus incident, the Planning Section helps ensure responders have accurate information, such as the number of students remaining in the building. We can also provide resources such as maps and floor plans. In addition to developing plans, we can provide an invaluable service by recording a chronology of incident events for legal, analytical, fiscal, and historical purposes.

| Topic | Planning Section |

Visual 5.24

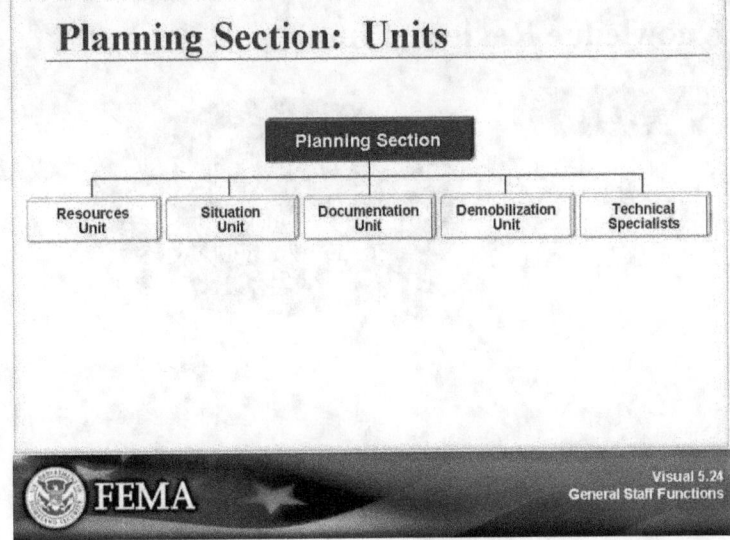

Visual Description: Planning Section: Units

Instructor Notes

Summarize the following key points:

The Planning Section can be further staffed with four Units. In addition, Technical Specialists who provide special expertise useful in incident management and response may also be assigned to work in the Planning Section. Depending on the needs, Technical Specialists may also be assigned to other Sections in the organization.

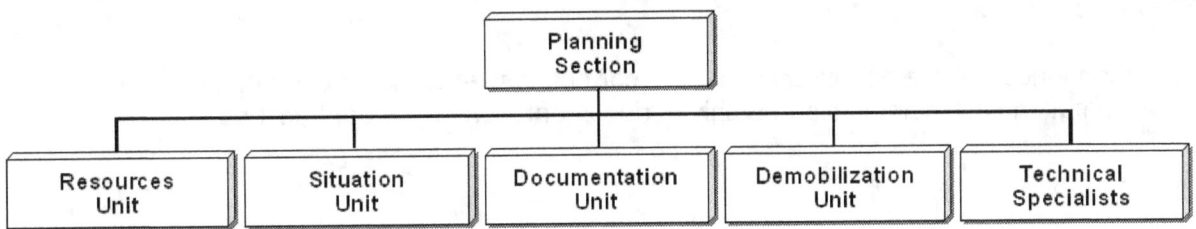

- **Resources Unit:** Conducts all check-in activities and maintains the status of all incident resources. The Resources Unit plays a significant role in preparing the written Incident Action Plan.
- **Situation Unit:** Collects and analyzes information on the current situation, prepares situation displays and situation summaries, and develops maps and projections.
- **Documentation Unit:** Provides duplication services, including the written Incident Action Plan. Maintains and archives all incident-related documentation.
- **Demobilization Unit:** Assists in ensuring that resources are released from the incident in an orderly, safe, and cost-effective manner.

Visual 5.25

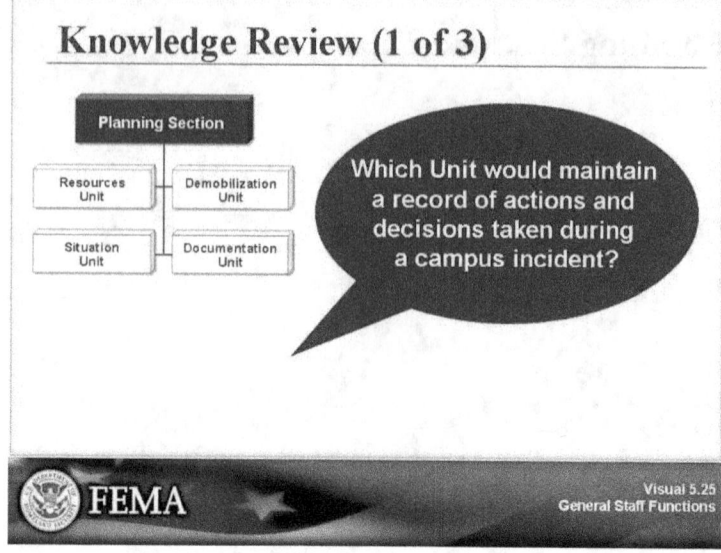

Visual Description: Knowledge Review (1 of 3) – Which Unit would maintain a record of actions taken during a campus incident? The options are Resources Unit, Demobilization Unit, Situation Unit, or Documentation Unit.

Instructor Notes

Ask the participants the following question:

Which Planning Section Unit would maintain a record of actions taken during a campus incident?

Allow time to respond.

If not mentioned, tell the participants that the correct answer is the Documentation Unit. The Documentation Unit maintains and archives documentation on incident actions.

| Topic | Knowledge Review |

Visual 5.26

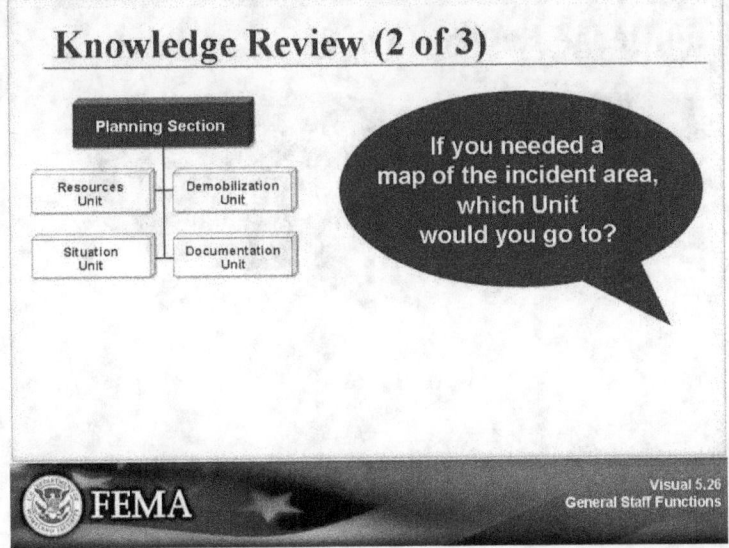

Visual Description: Knowledge Review (2 of 3) – If you needed a map of the incident area, which Unit would you go to? The options are Resources Unit, Demobilization Unit, Situation Unit, or Documentation Unit.

Instructor Notes

Ask the group the following question:

If you needed a map of the incident area, which Planning Section Unit would you go to?

Allow time to respond.

If not mentioned, tell the participants that the correct answer is the Situation Unit. The Situation Unit develops maps and projections and prepares situation displays and situation summaries.

Topic | **Knowledge Review**

Visual 5.27

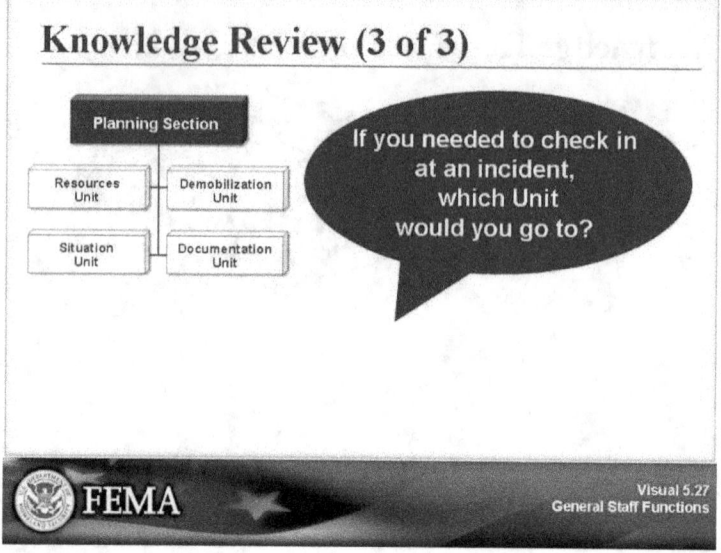

Visual Description: Knowledge Review (3 of 3) – If you needed to check in at an incident, which Unit would you go to? The options are Resources Unit, Demobilization Unit, Situation Unit, or Documentation Unit.

Instructor Notes

Ask the participants the following question:

If you needed to check in at an incident, which Planning Section Unit would you go to?

Allow time to respond.

If not mentioned, tell the participants that the correct answer is the Resources Unit. The Resources Unit conducts all check-in activities and maintains the status of all incident resources.

Topic	Logistics Section

Visual 5.28

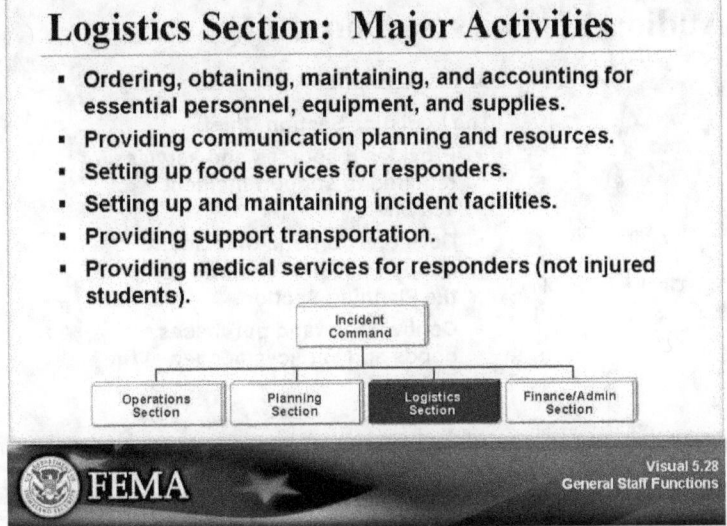

Visual Description: Logistics Section: Major Activities

Instructor Notes

Summarize the following key points:

The Logistics Section is responsible for all of the services and support needs, including:

- Ordering, obtaining, maintaining, and accounting for essential personnel, equipment, and supplies.
- Providing communication planning and resources.
- Setting up food services for responders.
- Setting up and maintaining incident facilities.
- Providing support transportation.
- Providing medical services to **incident personnel (not injured students).**

Topic	Logistics Section

Visual 5.29

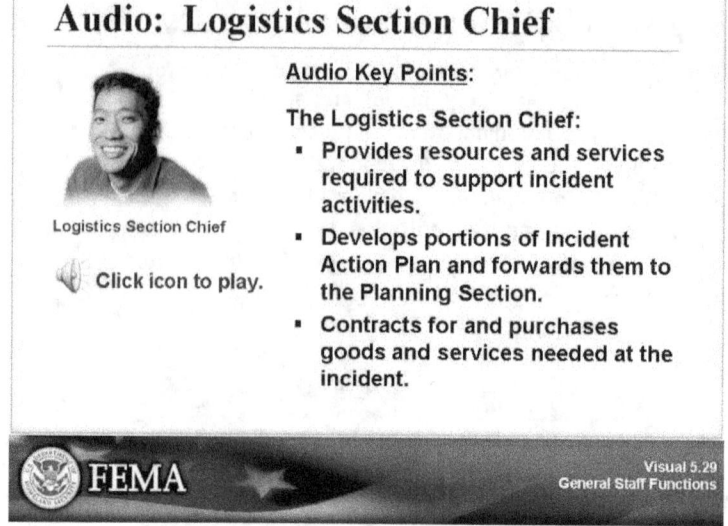

Visual Description: Audio: Logistics Section Chief

Instructor Notes

Summarize the following key points:

- The Incident Commander will determine if there is a need for a Logistics Section at the incident, and if so, will designate an individual to fill the position of the Logistics Section Chief.

- The Logistic Section Chief helps make sure that there are adequate resources (personnel, supplies, and equipment) for meeting the incident objectives.

Tell the participants that you will play a short audio of a Logistics Section Chief describing his role in the ICS organization.

Audio Transcript:

Logistics can make or break an incident response. I assist the Incident Commander and Operations Section Chief by providing the resources and services required to support incident activities. During an incident, Logistics is responsible for ensuring that there are sufficient food, water, and sanitation supplies. We are also responsible for arranging buses for evacuations and communication equipment.

Logistics and Finance have to work closely to contract for and purchase goods and services needed at the incident.

Visual 5.30

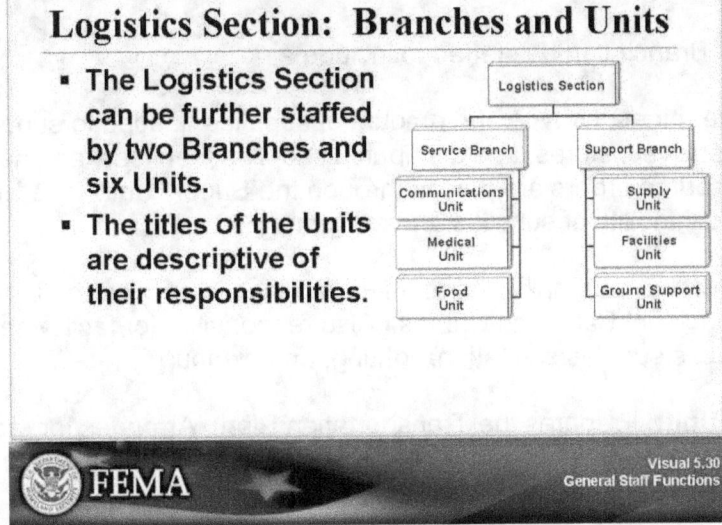

Visual Description: Logistics Section: Branches and Units

Instructor Notes

Summarize the following key points:

- The Logistics Section can be further staffed by two Branches and six Units.

- The titles of the Units are descriptive of their responsibilities.

Service Branch

The Logistics Service Branch can be staffed to include a:

- **Communications Unit:** Prepares and implements the Incident Communications Plan (ICS-205), distributes and maintains communications equipment, supervises the Incident Communications Center, and establishes adequate communications over the incident.

- **Medical Unit:** Develops the Medical Plan (ICS-206), provides first aid and light medical treatment for personnel assigned to the incident, and prepares procedures for a major medical emergency.

- **Food Unit:** Supplies the food and potable water for all incident facilities and personnel, and obtains the necessary equipment and supplies to operate food service facilities at Bases and Camps.

Support Branch

The Logistics Support Branch can be staffed to include a:

- **Supply Unit:** Determines the type and amount of supplies needed to support the incident. The Unit orders, receives, stores, and distributes supplies, services, and nonexpendable equipment. All resource orders are placed through the Supply Unit. The Unit maintains inventory and accountability of supplies and equipment.

- **Facilities Unit:** Sets up and maintains required facilities to support the incident. Provides managers for the Incident Base and Camps. Also responsible for facility security and facility maintenance services such as sanitation, lighting, and cleanup.

- **Ground Support Unit:** Prepares the Transportation Plan. Arranges for, activates, and documents the fueling, maintenance, and repair of ground resources. Arranges for the transportation of personnel, supplies, food, and equipment.

Topic	Finance/Administration Section

Visual 5.31

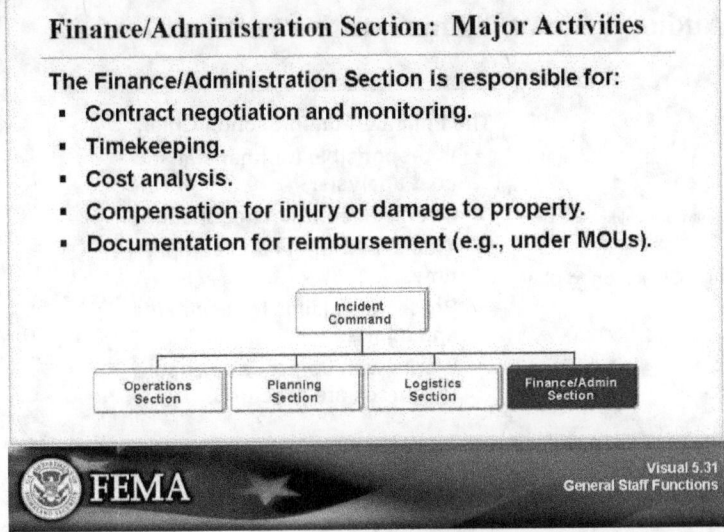

Visual Description: Finance/Administration Section: Major Activities

---

Instructor Notes

Summarize the following key points:

The Finance/Administration Section is set up for any incident that requires incident-specific financial management. The Finance/Administration Section is responsible for:

- Contract negotiation and monitoring.
- Timekeeping.
- Cost analysis.
- Compensation for injury or damage to property.
- Documentation for reimbursement (e.g., under Memorandums of Understanding (MOUs)).

Topic | **Finance/Administration Section**

Visual 5.32

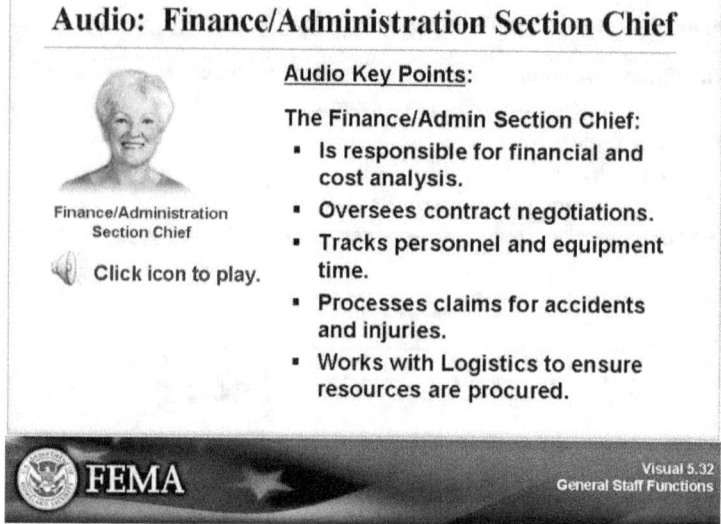

Visual Description: Audio: Finance/Administration Section Chief

---

Instructor Notes

Summarize the following key points:

The Incident Commander will determine if there is a need for a Finance/Administration Section at the incident, and if so, will designate an individual to fill the position of the Finance/Administration Section Chief.

Tell the participants you will play a short audio of a Finance/Administration Section Chief describing her role in the ICS organization.

Audio Transcript:

I'm the one who worries about paying for the response efforts. I'm responsible for all of the financial and cost analysis aspects of an incident. These include contract negotiation, tracking personnel and equipment time, documenting and processing claims for accidents and injuries occurring at the incident, and keeping a running tally of the costs associated with the incident. I work most closely with Logistics to be sure that we are able to contract for and procure the resources necessary to manage an incident.

Visual 5.33

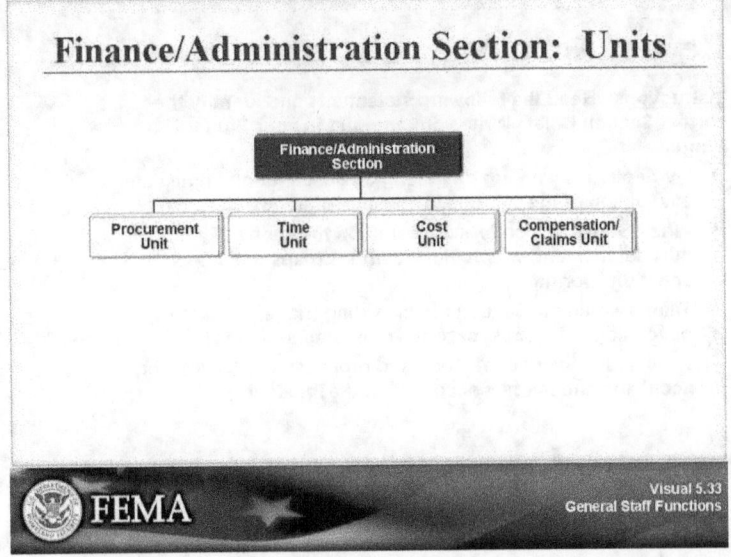

Visual Description: Finance/Administration Section: Units

Instructor Notes

Summarize the following key points:

- **Procurement Unit:** Responsible for administering all financial matters pertaining to vendor contracts, leases, and fiscal agreements.

- **Time Unit:** Responsible for incident personnel time recording.

- **Cost Unit:** Collects all cost data, performs cost effectiveness analyses, provides cost estimates, and makes cost savings recommendations.

- **Compensation/Claims Unit:** Responsible for the overall management and direction of all administrative matters pertaining to compensation for injury-related and claims-related activities kept for the incident.

Topic	Review Activity

Visual 5.34

Review Activity

Instructions: Read the following statements and identify the correct Section Chief. Write your answers in your Student Manual.

- My Section is working on getting 50 buses for an immediate evacuation of the campus in advance of floodwaters.
- When SWAT responders appeared on the scene of a hostile intruder incident, we provided campus maps and class schedules for the day.
- Teams within my Section are providing triage, treatment, and psychological first aid services to injured students.
- We oversee the documenting and processing of claims for accidents and injuries occurring at the incident.

FEMA

Visual 5.34
General Staff Functions

Visual Description: Review Activity

Instructor Notes

Instructions: Use the following activity to review the General Staff Section responsibilities. Ask the participants to identify the correct Section Chief.

	Statement	Which Section?
A	My Section is working on getting 50 buses for an immediate evacuation of the campus in advance of floodwaters.	
B	When SWAT responders appeared on the scene of a hostile intruder incident, we provided campus maps and class schedules for the day.	
C	Teams within my Section are providing triage, treatment, and psychological first-aid services to injured students.	
D	We oversee the documenting and processing of claims for accidents and injuries occurring at the incident.	

Ask for volunteers to identify the correct Section Chief for each statement. If not mentioned, tell the participants that the correct answers are:

A. Logistics Section Chief
B. Planning Section Chief
C. Operations Section Chief
D. Finance/Administration Section Chief

Topic	Case Study: General Staff Functions

Visual 5.35

Case Study: General Staff Functions

Instructions:

1. Working as a team, review the case study presented in your Student Manuals.

2. Use what you've learned to answer the questions in your Student Manuals. Write your answers on chart paper.

3. Select a spokesperson and be prepared to discuss with the class in 15 minutes.

FEMA

Visual 5.35
General Staff Functions

Visual Description: Case Study: General Staff Functions

Instructor Notes

Provide the following instructions to the participants for the case study.

Instructions:

1. Working as a team, review the case study presented in your Student Manuals.
2. Use what you've learned to answer the questions for each part of the case study before proceeding to the next page. Write your answers on chart paper.
3. When you've answered each set of questions, move on to the next page.
4. Select a spokesperson and be prepared to discuss your answers to all the questions in 15 minutes.

Scenario Part 1: A graduate student discovers a package leaking mercury in a campus laboratory classroom. The label on the box indicates it was shipped from another local university, but no one is sure how long the box has been there, or how long it has been leaking. The student notifies a faculty member, who establishes the initial ICS organization.

Question:

In the ICS organization described above, the faculty member has assumed which role?

| Topic | Case Study Part 2 |

Scenario Part 2: The faculty member calls campus public safety. Shortly afterward, the campus police chief arrives at the scene, along with one of her officers. HazMat responders from the local fire department on are their way.

Questions:

- **What must happen before the police chief assumes the Incident Commander role?**

- **What is the police officer in the ICS organization?**

Scenario Part 3: A transfer of command occurs and the police chief assumes the Incident Commander role. The Command and General Staff positions are filled as shown on the chart.

Questions:

- **Does the Incident Commander have a manageable span of control?**

- **What is the title of the person in charge of the Perimeter Security Strike Team?**

- **What member of the Command Staff would go in the box with the question mark?**

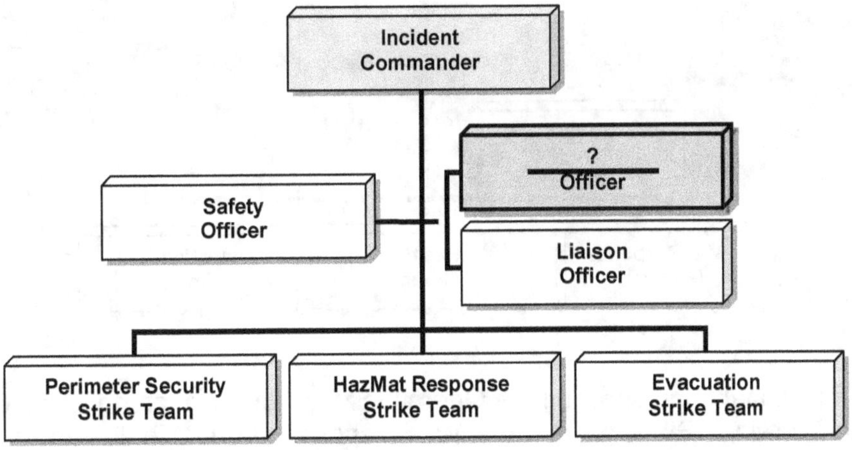

Caption: Organizational chart with Incident Commander, Safety Officer, [?] Officer, Liaison Officer, Perimeter Security Strike Team, HazMat Response Strike Team, and Evacuation Strike Team.

Topic	Case Study Part 4

Scenario Part 4: To maintain span of control as the incident expands, the Incident Commander establishes an Operations Section.

Questions:

- **What is the role of the Operations Section?**

- **What is the ICS title of the person in charge of the Operations Section?**

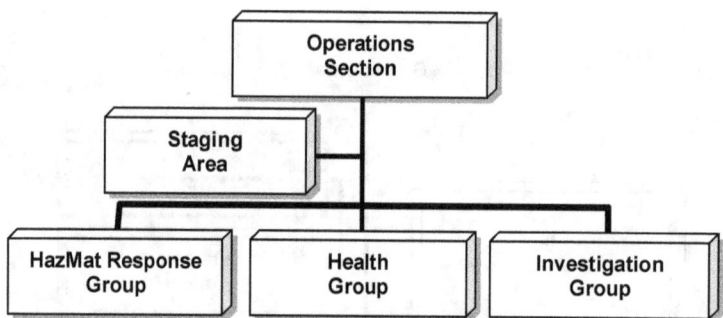

Caption: Organizational chart showing the Operations Section. Reporting to the Operations Section are the following: Staging Area, HazMat Response Group, Health Group, and Investigation Group.

| Topic | Case Study Part 5 |

Scenario Part 5: After the first hour, the Incident Commander establishes a second Section that will develop the Incident Action Plan and track the status of resources on the scene.

Question:

- **What is the correct title of this Section?**

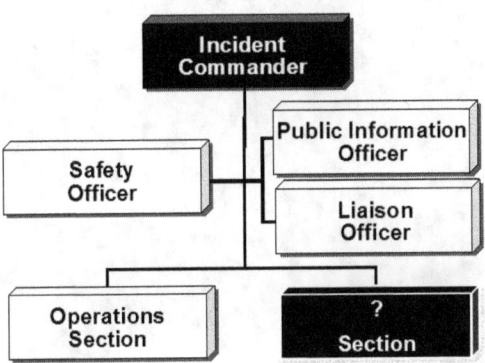

Caption: Organizational chart with Incident Commander, Command Staff, and Operations Section. A second Section has been added.

Topic   **Case Study Part 6**

<u>Scenario Part 6</u>: Because it remains unclear how long the package has been leaking, there is a need to find students and staff who may have come in contact with the mercury. Given the number of personnel on the scene, there is a need to provide meals, food, first aid, and rest areas for responders.

<u>Question</u>:

Which Section is responsible for providing these support resources?

Scenario Part 7: It is determined that the package was delivered through the campus mail service several hours earlier, and the spill was discovered during the first class of the day. No traces of mercury are found in the campus mail facility. Cleanup in the lab is complete, and the few exposed students and staff have been located and are undergoing treatment.

Question:

Which resources would you demobilize first? Why?

Topic	Case Study Debrief

Instructions: Monitor the time. After 15 minutes has passed, ask the groups to present their answers. If not mentioned by participants, provided the following correct answers:

In the ICS organization described above, the faculty member has assumed which role?
The Incident Commander. The faculty member was the first on the scene and was responsible for establishing the initial ICS organization. He or she was functioning as the Incident Commander.

What must happen before the police chief assumes the Incident Commander role? *There must be a transfer of command briefing for the incoming Incident Commander. In this case, the police chief must be briefed by the faculty member.*

What is the police officer in the ICS organization? *The police officer is a Single Resource in the ICS organization.*

Does the Incident Commander have a manageable span of control? *The Incident Commander does have a manageable span of control.*

What is the title of the person in charge of the Perimeter Security Strike Team? *A Leader would be in charge of the Perimeter Security Strike Team.*

What member of the Command Staff should go in the box with the question mark? *The Public Information Officer is the other member of the Command Staff.*

What is the role of the Operations Section? *The Operations Section directs and controls all tactical operations for the incident.*

What is the ICS title of the person in charge of the Operations Section? *The correct title of the person in charge of the Operations Section is "Chief."*

What is the correct title of the Section in Part 5?
If not mentioned, tell the participants that the correct answer is the Planning Section. As part of its many responsibilities, the Planning Section prepares and documents the Incident Action Plan (IAP).

Which Section is responsible for providing the support resources described in Part 6?
If not mentioned, tell the participants that the correct answer is the Logistics Section. As part of its responsibilities, the Logistics Section is responsible for all services and support needs, such as food and medical services.

Which resources would you demobilize first? Why?
There is no single correct answer. Use this activity as an opportunity to have the participants think about the need for demobilization planning. Some of the factors that should be considered during the demobilization of this incident include: continued need for investigative resources, continued media coverage, recognition of volunteers, etc.

Topic   Summary

Visual 5.36

Summary

Are you able to describe the roles and functions of the:

- Operations Section?
- Planning Section?
- Logistics Section?
- Finance/Administration Section?

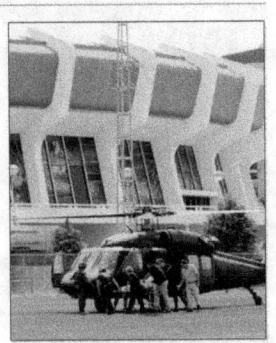

FEMA

Visual 5.36
General Staff Functions

Visual Description: Summary

Instructor Notes

Ask the participants if they are able to describe the roles and functions of the:

- Operations Section.
- Planning Section.
- Logistics Section.
- Finance/Administration Section.

Ask if anyone has any questions about anything covered in this unit.

The next unit will focus on the features and organizational structures related to Unified Command.

Your Notes:

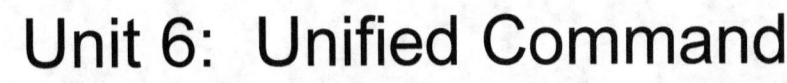

Unit 6: Unified Command

Objectives

At the end of this unit, the participants should be able to:

- Define Unified Command.
- List the advantages of Unified Command.
- Identify the primary features of Unified Command.
- Describe the roles and reporting relationships between campus personnel and emergency responders under a Unified Command.

Scope

- Unit Introduction
- Unit Overview
- Activity: Optimal Strategy
- Unified Command Definition and Benefits
- Unified Command Features
- Unified Command Organization
- Unified Command Strategies
- Case Study: Unified Command
- Quick Reference Guide: ICS Organization
- Quick Reference Guide: Position Titles
- Summary

Methodology

The instructors will review the objectives for this unit and then provide an overview of Unified Command. A case study involving a student demonstration will be used to illustrate the benefits of Unified Command.

Next the instructors will present the features and organizational structures related to Unified Command. Participants will work in teams to apply Unified Command principles in a case study exercise. Two quick reference guides are included in this unit—ICS Organization and Position Titles—that participants can use on the job.

The instructors will then transition to the next unit that focuses on putting together the information learned in this course to prepare to implement ICS.

Time Plan

A suggested time plan for this unit is shown below. More or less time may be required, based on the experience level of the group.

Topic	Time
Unit Introduction and Unit Overview	5 minutes
Activity: Optimal Strategy	5 minutes
Unified Command Definition and Benefits	5 minutes
Unified Command Features	2 minutes
Unified Command Organization	5 minutes
Unified Command Strategies	5 minutes
Case Study: Unified Command	25 minutes
Summary	3 minutes
Total Time	**55 minutes**

| Topic | Unit Introduction |

Visual 6.1

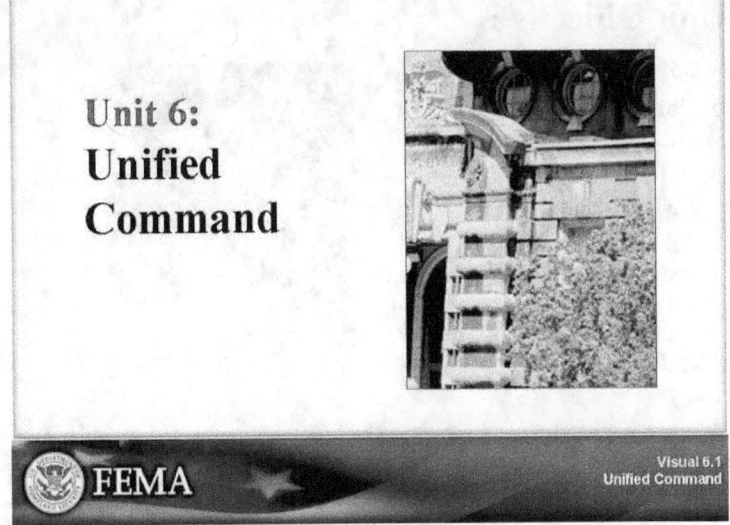

Visual Description: Unit Introduction

Instructor Notes

Present the following key content:

- The previous units covered the Incident Command Systems (ICS) fundamentals. This unit introduces you to a more advanced concept, called **Unified Command**.

- Unified Command:
  - Applies ICS in incidents involving multiple jurisdictions or agencies.
  - Enables institutions and agencies with different legal, geographic, and functional responsibilities to coordinate, plan, and interact effectively.

Topic	Unit Objectives

Visual 6.2

Unit Objectives

- Define Unified Command.
- List the advantages of Unified Command.
- Identify the primary features of Unified Command.
- Describe the roles and reporting relationships between campus personnel and emergency responders under a Unified Command.

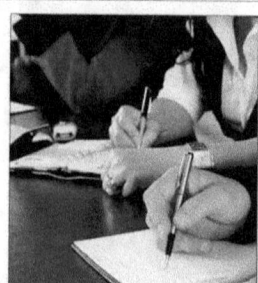

FEMA

Visual 6.2
Unified Command

Visual Description: Unit Objectives

Instructor Notes

Tell the participants that by the end of this lesson, they should be able to:

- Define Unified Command.
- List the advantages of Unified Command.
- Identify the primary features of Unified Command.
- Describe the roles and reporting relationships between campus personnel and emergency responders under a Unified Command.

Topic	Activity: Optimal Strategy

Visual 6.3

Activity: Optimal Strategy

Instructions: Read the scenario below and select the optimal strategy in your Student Manual.

Scenario: A political protest started on campus and has spread into the surrounding community, with student and nonstudent demonstrators defacing campus, city, and private property, setting fires, and disrupting traffic. Protestors have overturned a vehicle at the entrance to the campus, and taken hostages in a building that contains a bank on the first floor and campus administrative offices on upper floors.

FEMA

Visual 6.3
Unified Command

Visual Description: Activity: Optimal Strategy

Instructor Notes

Instructions: Read the scenario below and select the optimal strategy that provides the best solution.

Scenario: A political protest started on campus and has spread into the surrounding community, with student and nonstudent demonstrators defacing campus, city, and private property, setting fires, and disrupting traffic. Protestors have overturned a vehicle at the entrance to the campus, and have taken hostages in a building that contains a bank on the first floor and campus administrative offices on upper floors.

Select the optimal strategy.

☐ Divide the incident along geographic and functional lines so that each county, the State, and the institution can establish its own ICS organization with well-defined areas of responsibilities.

☐ Create a single ICS incident structure that allows for an effective multijurisdictional or multiagency approach.

Allow the participants time to select a strategy. Facilitate a discussion. If not mentioned by the participants, make the following points:

Unified Command: The preferred solution is to **create a single ICS incident structure with a built-in process for an effective and responsible multijurisdictional or multiagency approach.** This solution became Unified Command.

Separate Commands: The other option of dividing the incident into separate command structures may be the simplest political solution but is often not effective. If separate commands were used, there is a danger of:

- Critical life-safety incident objectives being missed because each command assumed that another one was taking responsibility.
- Duplication of efforts and competing for the same scarce resources.
- Inconsistent messages being reported to the media and parents.

Topic	Unified Command Definition and Benefits

Visual 6.4

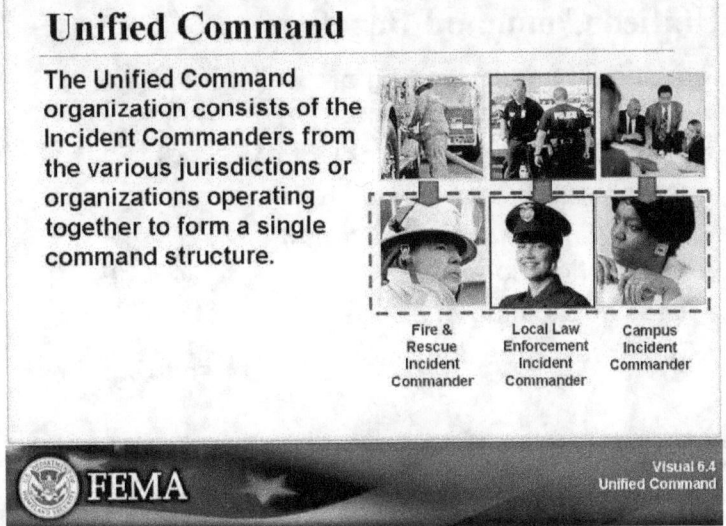

Visual Description: Unified Command

Instructor Notes

Unified Command:

- Applies ICS in incidents involving multiple jurisdictions or organizations.
- Enables institutions and agencies with different legal, geographic, and functional responsibilities to coordinate, plan, and interact effectively.

The Incident Commanders within the Unified Command make joint decisions and speak as one voice. Any differences are worked out within the Unified Command.

Unity of command is maintained. Each responder reports to a single supervisor within his or her area of expertise. Within a Unified Command the police officer would not tell the firefighters how to do their job nor would the police tell campus personnel how to notify students of a campus incident.

| Topic | Unified Command Definition and Benefits |

Visual 6.5

Unified Command Benefits

- A shared understanding of priorities and restrictions.
- A single set of incident objectives.
- Collaborative strategies.
- Improved internal and external information flow.
- Less duplication of efforts.
- Better resource utilization.

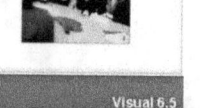
FEMA

Visual 6.5
Unified Command

Visual Description: Unified Command Benefits

Instructor Notes

Explain that in a Unified Command, institutions and responding agencies blend into an integrated, unified team. A unified approach results in:

- A shared understanding of priorities and restrictions.
- A single set of incident objectives.
- Collaborative strategies.
- Improved internal and external information flow.
- Less duplication of efforts
- Better resource utilization.

Topic	Unified Command Features

Visual 6.6

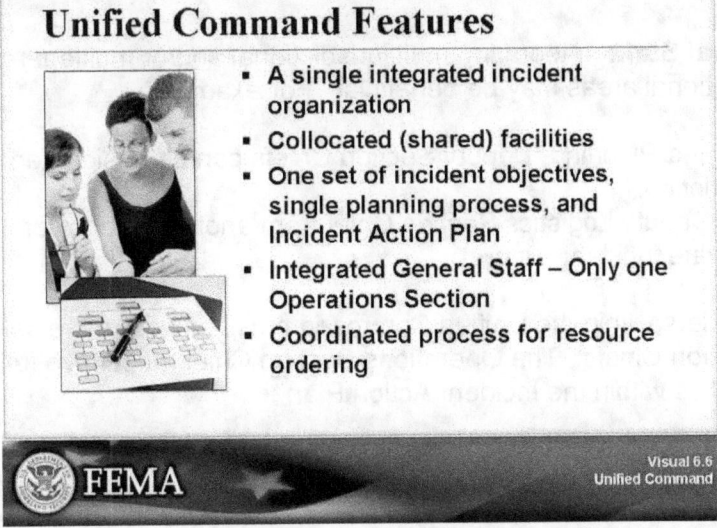

Visual Description: Unified Command Features

Instructor Notes

Review the following features of Unified Command:

- **A Single Integrated Incident Organization:** As a team effort, Unified Command overcomes much of the inefficiency and duplication of effort that can occur when agencies from different functional and geographic jurisdictions, or agencies at different levels of government, operate without a common system or organizational framework.

- **Collocated (Shared) Facilities:** In a Unified Command incident facilities are collocated or shared. There is one single Incident Command Post.

- **One Set of Incident Objectives, Single Planning Process, and Incident Action Plan:** Unified Command uses one set of incident objectives and a single planning process, and produces one Incident Action Plan (IAP). The planning process for Unified Command is similar to the process used on single jurisdiction incidents.

Topic   **Unified Command Features**

Continue reviewing the following features of Unified Command:

- **Integrated General Staff:** Integrating multijurisdictional and/or multiagency personnel into various other functional areas may be beneficial. For example:

  - In Operations and Planning, Deputy Section Chiefs can be designated from an adjacent jurisdiction.
  - In Logistics, a Deputy Logistics Section Chief from another agency or jurisdiction can help to coordinate incident support.

  Incident Commanders within the Unified Command must concur on the selection of the General Staff Section Chiefs. The Operations Section Chief must have full authority to implement the tactics within the Incident Action Plan.

- **Coordinated Process for Resource Ordering:** The Incident Commanders within the Unified Command work together to establish resource ordering procedures that allow for:

  - Deployment of scarce resources to meet high-priority objectives.
  - Potential cost savings through agreements on cost sharing for essential services.

Topic	Unified Command Organization

Visual 6.7

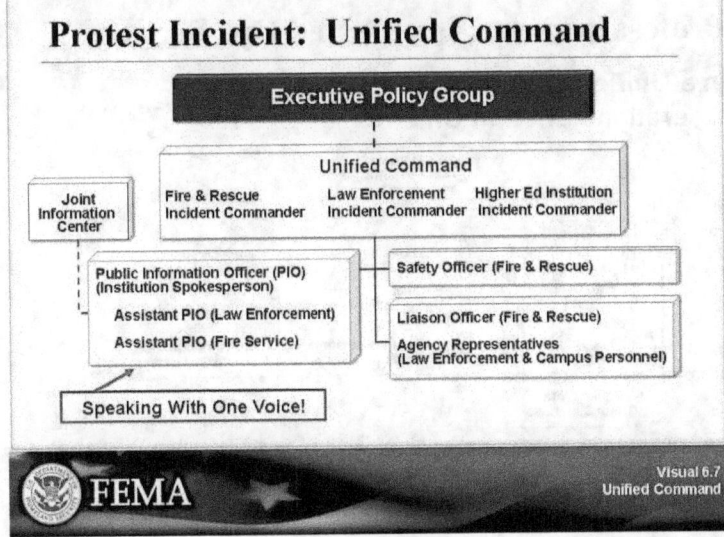

Visual Description: Protest Incident: Unified Command

Instructor Notes

Unified Command results in a single integrated incident organization. Below is a sample Command Staff organizational chart for a political protest that started on campus and spread to the surrounding community, with demonstrations quickly developing into widespread destruction. Notice that the Unified Command is composed of the agencies involved: Fire & Rescue, Law Enforcement, and Institution, and that personnel from the different agencies often are assigned as Assistant Officers.

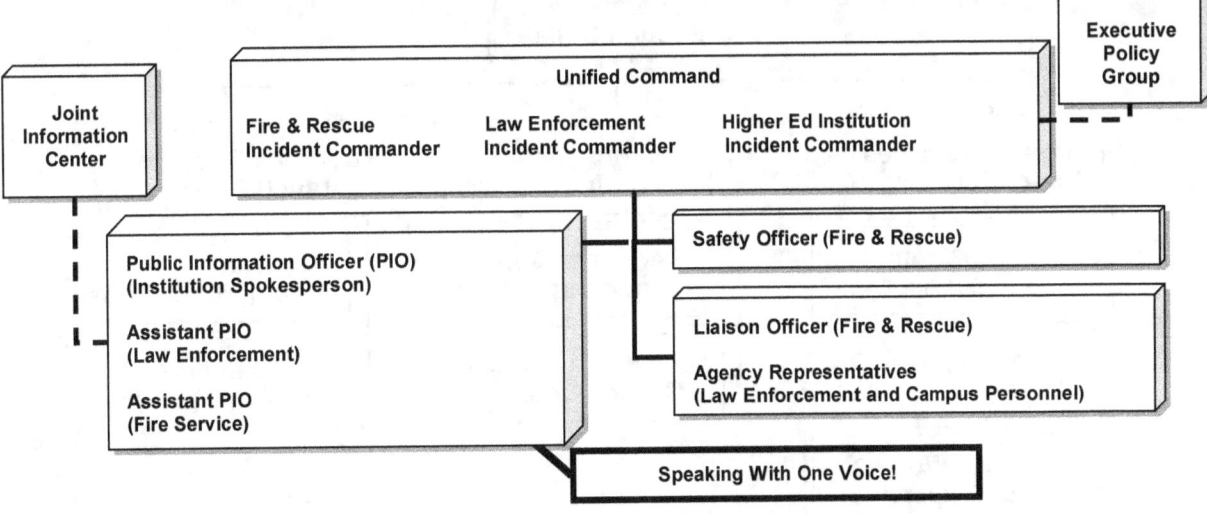

The combined Public Information approach ensures that the responders will speak with one voice.

Visual 6.8

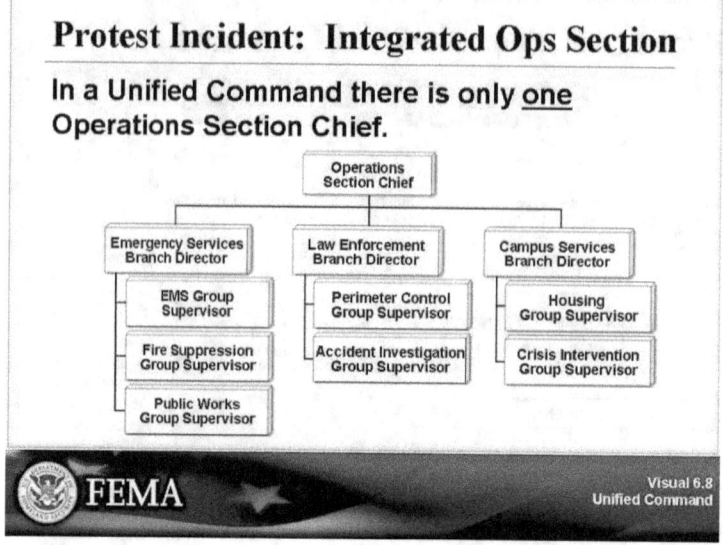

Visual Description: Protest Incident: Integrated Ops Section

Instructor Notes

In a Unified Command there is only one Operations Section Chief. The Operations Section Chief should be the most qualified and experienced person available. Below is a sample Operations Section organizational chart for a campus incident.

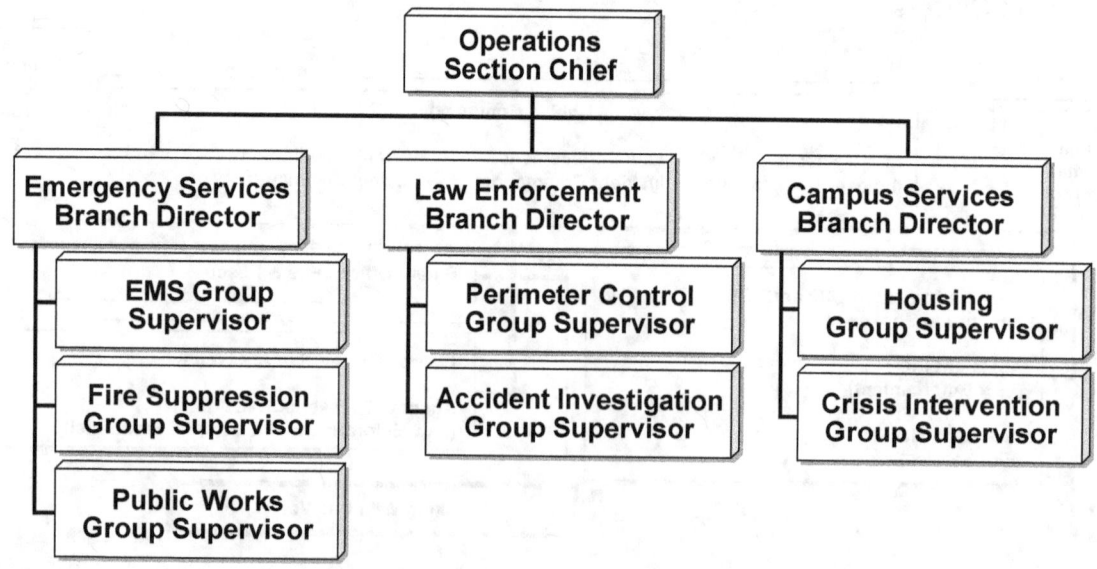

Topic	Unified Command Strategies

Visual 6.9

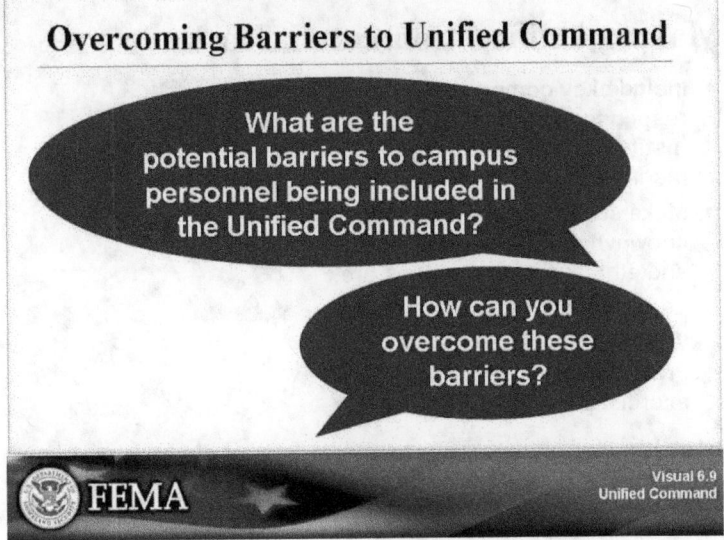

Visual Description: Overcoming Barriers to Unified Command

Instructor Notes

Facilitate a group discussion using the following discussion questions:

What are the potential barriers to campus personnel being included in the Unified Command?

How can you overcome these barriers?

Proceed to the next slide for a discussion of ways to overcome barriers and make Unified Command work.

| Topic | Unified Command Strategies |

Visual 6.10

Making Unified Command Work

- Include key community response personnel in your institution's emergency planning process.
- Make sure that first responders know what the institution's legal and ethical responsibilities are.
- Learn ICS so that you can blend into the response structure.
- Practice together during exercises and planned events.

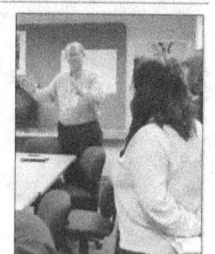

FEMA

Visual 6.10
Unified Command

Visual Description: Making Unified Command Work

Instructor Notes

For Unified Command to be used successfully, it is important that institutions and agencies prepare by:

- Including key community response personnel in your institution's planning process.

- Making sure that first responders know what the institution's legal and ethical responsibilities are during an event.

- Learning ICS so that they can blend into the response structure.

- Practicing together during exercises and planned events.

Tell the participants to turn to the next page for testimonials from three people who were involved in Unified Command situations at higher education institutions.

Topic	Unified Command Strategies

Visual 6.11

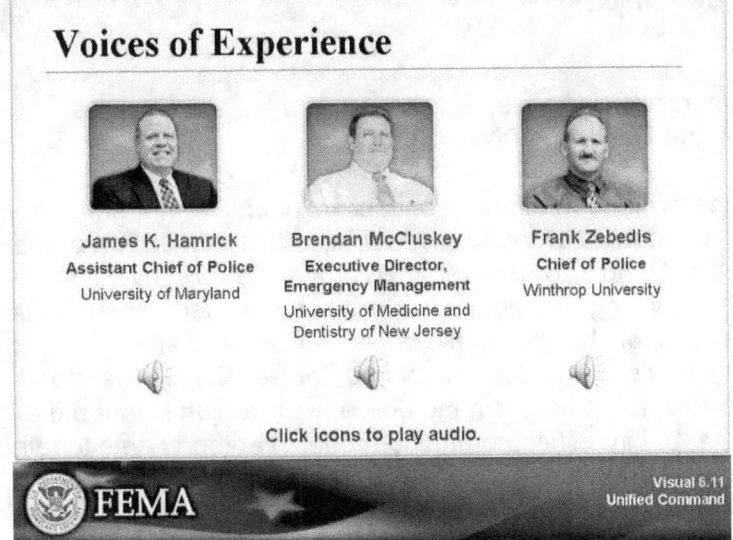

Visual Description: Voices of Experience

Instructor Notes

Tell the participants they will be hearing "voices of experience" from three campus personnel about the use of Unified Command.

Click on each icon to hear the "voice of experience."

Audio Transcripts:

James K. Hamrick
Assistant Chief of Police
University of Maryland

I think that communication is a vitally important element of the Incident Command System because if you look at lessons learned from just about every major critical incident that has been debriefed around the country, you are going to find that communication is near the top of the list, some element of breakdown in communication in terms of that incident and so communication becomes an important element of the Incident Command System in being able to talk across different agencies that may be represented in the response of that and being able to manage the flow of information both down and up the incident command structure and then the flow of information to any coordinating agency such as an emergency operations center as well as a policy group, Presidents, Vice Presidents, Provost of the institution who have an interest in continuity of operations for the institution.

Audio Transcripts: (Continued)

Brendan McCluskey
Executive Director, Emergency Management
University of Medicine and Dentistry of New Jersey

Unified command is somewhat of a difficult concept for people to understand because while no individual Incident Commander is giving up control over their jurisdiction or their assets. They all need to come together to work toward common goals and objectives. While we have this group of people together making decisions, essentially the unified command is acting as a conglomeration and as a single body to make decisions. Essentially they become the Incident Commander and I think that's a very difficult concept for people to understand because if you're a police officer and you traditionally command police, you wouldn't want a firefighter saying what to, what should be done, but in unified command model everybody gets together and collectively makes those important decisions.

Frank Zebedis
Chief of Police
Winthrop University

Basically you are dealing with different agencies, different disciplines coming together as the scene unfolds. You're going to have an Incident Commander who is going to be in charge but as other agencies get involved and other special entities are required or needed then that Incident Commander goes into what is called unified command, and at that point the different agencies and entities come together and they work in a very understanding environment to solve the situation or resolve the scene and nobody gives up their authority because if I'm fire, I'm the expert in the fire field. If I'm law enforcement, I'm the expert in the law enforcement field. I don't tell firefighters how to do their job; they don't tell me how to do my job as a police officer; so we look to each other for assistance and the professional in that field do what they need to do.

Topic	Case Study: Unified Command

Visual 6.12

Case Study: Unified Command

Instructions:

1. Working as a team, review the scenario located in your Student Manual.
2. Answer the questions in your Student Manual about the Unified Command structure.
3. Refer to the quick reference guides in your Student Manuals as needed.
4. Select a spokesperson and be prepared to present your work in 20 minutes.

FEMA

Visual 6.12
Unified Command

Visual Description: Case Study: Unified Command

Instructor Notes

Introduce the exercise by telling the participants that the scenario involves a political protest that starts on campus and spreads to the surrounding community. Note that the exercise applies the key learning points and the objectives for this unit.

Follow the steps below to conduct this exercise:

1. Divide the participants into teams.
2. Review the scenario with the participants, referring them to the following pages in their Student Manuals.
3. Tell the participants to select a spokesperson and be prepared to present to the class in 20 minutes.
4. Note that participants may refer to the quick reference guides in their Student Manuals as needed.

Debrief: Monitor the time. After 20 minutes, conduct a debrief as follows:

1. Ask one team to present who they would include in the Unified Command structure.
2. Ask the other teams if they had different responses. Compare the similarities and differences among the teams. There is no one correct answer.
3. Next, ask a different team to present their answer to the next question. After the team presents, ask the other teams to comment. Continue with this process until all teams have presented.
4. Summarize the key learning points. Make sure to provide any needed guidance or correct any misunderstandings or inaccurate application of ICS principles and concepts.

Topic	Case Study: Unified Command

Instructions:

1. Working in teams, review the scenario on the next page in your Student Manuals.

2. Assuming that a Unified Command will be established (see the quick reference guides following the exercise for assistance), answer the following questions:

   - **Which agencies/organizations should be included in the Unified Command structure?**

   - **Which ICS positions/Sections will be activated?**

   - **How many Operations Section Chiefs will be assigned representing each of the agencies?**

   - **What is one example of an incident objective that the Unified Command group might establish?**

3. Select a spokesperson and be prepared to present your work in 20 minutes.

Topic	Case Study: Scenario

- Warehime University is a large, urban campus in the middle of a major metropolitan area, with approximately 20,000 undergraduate students and 10,000 graduate students. About 5,000 students live in campus residence halls, while the rest live in surrounding neighborhoods. Two major roads to the city's downtown area run straight through the campus.

- It is midafternoon on a warm weekday in March. Classes are in session, and tour groups of high-school seniors and their parents are walking through campus before making acceptance decisions for the following fall semester.

- A student political demonstration that started calmly on the lawn in front of the student union is rapidly growing more and more disorderly. Professional protesters and members of anarchist alliances have joined the initial group of students, many of them wearing masks or handkerchiefs to obscure their identity.

- The protest spreads across campus and into the surrounding community, with student and nonstudent demonstrators defacing campus, city, and private property, setting multiple fires, and disrupting traffic.

- In an attempt to restore order, public safety officials disperse tear gas on the crowd, without anticipating that it would be sucked into the ventilation system for a residence hall that houses 800 freshmen students. Students inside have begun complaining of the effects.

- Protestors overturned a vehicle in the middle of one of the roads leading to and from downtown, and then set the vehicle on fire. The vehicle fire has blocked all traffic just as rush hour is beginning.

- A small group of armed protesters has taken hostages in a building that houses a bank on the first floor and campus administrative offices on upper floors. The protestors object to the institution's acceptance of research grants related to the U.S. military and have demanded to speak with university officials.

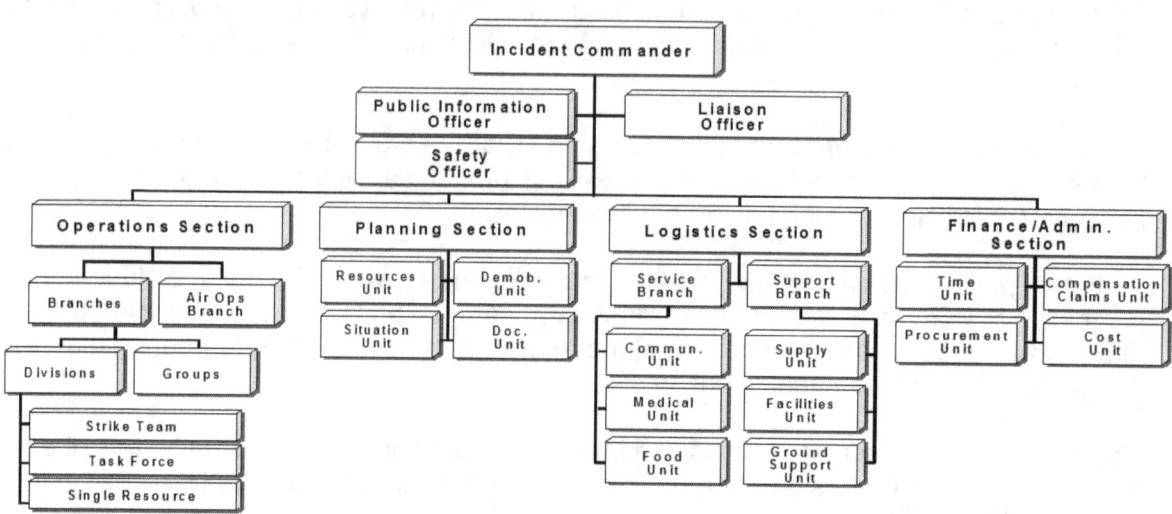

- **Command Staff:** The Command Staff consists of the Public Information Officer, Safety Officer, and Liaison Officer. They report directly to the Incident Commander.

- **Section:** The organization level having functional responsibility for primary segments of incident management (Operations, Planning, Logistics, Finance/Administration). The Section level is organizationally between Branch and Incident Commander.

- **Branch:** That organizational level having functional, geographical, or jurisdictional responsibility for major parts of the incident operations. The Branch level is organizationally between Section and Division/Group in the Operations Section, and between Section and Units in the Logistics Section. Branches are identified by the use of Roman Numerals, by function, or by jurisdictional name.

- **Division:** That organizational level having responsibility for operations within a defined geographic area. The Division level is organizationally between the Strike Team and the Branch.

- **Group:** Groups are established to divide the incident into functional areas of operation. Groups are located between Branches (when activated) and Resources in the Operations Section.

- **Unit:** That organization element having functional responsibility for a specific incident planning, logistics, or finance/administration activity.

- **Task Force:** A group of resources with common communications and a leader that may be pre-established and sent to an incident, or formed at an incident.

- **Strike Team:** Specified combinations of the same kind and type of resources, with common communications and a leader.

- **Single Resource:** An individual piece of equipment and its personnel complement, or an established crew or team of individuals with an identified work supervisor that can be used on an incident.

At each level within the ICS organization, individuals with primary responsibility positions have distinct titles. Titles provide a common standard for all users. For example, if one agency uses the title Branch Chief, another Branch Manager, etc., this lack of consistency can cause confusion at the incident.

The use of distinct titles for ICS positions allows for filling ICS positions with the most qualified individuals rather than by seniority. Standardized position titles are useful when requesting qualified personnel. For example, in deploying personnel, it is important to know if the positions needed are Unit Leaders, clerks, etc.

Listed below are the standard ICS titles:

Organizational Level	Title	Support Position
Incident Command	Incident Commander	Deputy
Command Staff	Officer	Assistant
General Staff (Section)	Chief	Deputy
Branch	Director	Deputy
Division/Group	Supervisor	N/A
Unit	Leader	Manager
Strike Team/Task Force	Leader	Single Resource Boss

Visual 6.13

Summary

Are you now able to:
- Define Unified Command?
- List the advantages of Unified Command?
- Identify the primary features of Unified Command?
- Describe the roles and reporting relationships between campus personnel and emergency responders under a Unified Command?

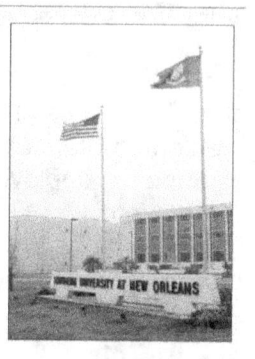

FEMA

Visual 6.13
Unified Command

Visual Description: Summary

Instructor Notes

Ask participants if they can now:

- Define Unified Command.
- List the advantages of Unified Command.
- Identify the primary features of Unified Command.
- Describe the roles and reporting relationships between campus personnel and emergency responders under a Unified Command.

Summarize this unit by reminding the group of the following:

The purpose of this lesson was to familiarize you with Unified Command features. Additional ICS training is required to prepare you to implement Unified Command.

Remember that Unified Command:
- Applies ICS in incidents involving multiple jurisdictions or agencies.
- Enables institutions and agencies with different legal, geographic, and functional responsibilities to coordinate, plan, and interact effectively.

Ask if anyone has any questions about anything covered in this unit.

The next unit focuses on putting together the information learned in this course to prepare to implement ICS.

Unit 7: Course Summary – Putting It All Together

Objectives

At the end of this unit, the participants should be able to:

- Describe the steps to take to ensure they are ready to assume ICS responsibilities.
- Assess their institution's readiness for implementing ICS.
- Take the final exam.

Scope

- Unit Introduction
- Unit Objectives
- Making ICS Work!
- Recordkeeping and Demobilization
- Voices of Experience
- Preparedness
- Taking the Exam and Feedback

Methodology

The final unit begins with emphasis on the personal actions that each person must take to make ICS work. The unit then covers recordkeeping and demobilization. Next, the instructors will discuss how to assess an institution's preparedness for implementing ICS. The instructors will then provide instructions on taking the final exam. To conclude the unit, the instructors will emphasize to the group the importance of providing course feedback.

Time Plan

A suggested time plan for this unit is shown below. More or less time may be required, based on the experience level of the group.

Topic	Time
Unit Introduction and Unit Objectives	5 minutes
Making ICS Work!	5 minutes
Recordkeeping and Demobilization	5 minutes
Voices of Experience	10 minutes
Preparedness	10 minutes
Taking the Exam and Feedback	10 minutes
Final Exam	30 minutes
Total Time	**1 hour 15 minutes**

This page intentionally left blank.

| Topic | Unit Introduction |

Visual 7.1

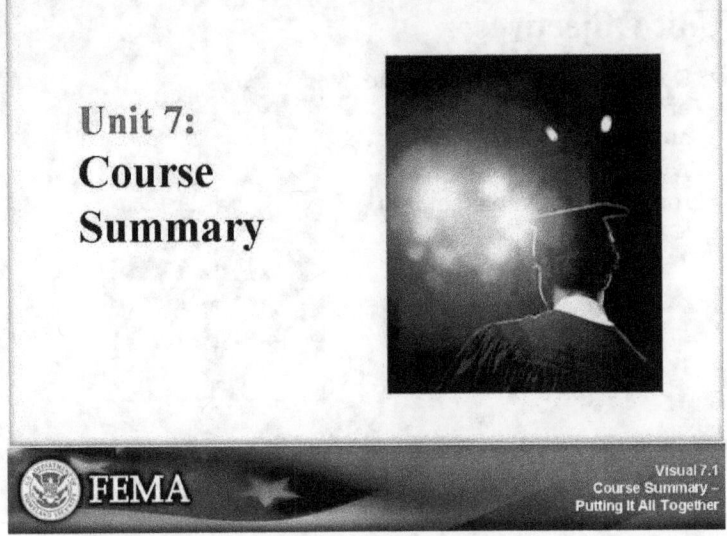

Visual Description: Unit Introduction

Instructor Notes

Explain that participants should now be familiar with the core system features of ICS and the ICS organizational roles and responsibilities.

Explain that "putting it all together" means that:

- You are personally ready to follow the ICS principles.
- Your campus is ready to implement ICS.

| Topic | Unit Objectives |

Visual 7.2

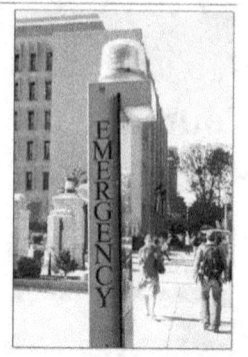

Unit Objectives

- Describe the steps to take to ensure you are ready to assume ICS responsibilities.
- Assess your institution's readiness for implementing ICS.
- Take the final exam.

FEMA

Visual 7.2
Course Summary –
Putting It All Together

Visual Description: Unit Objectives

Instructor Notes

Tell the participants that by the end of this unit, they should be able to:

- Describe the steps to take to ensure you are ready to assume ICS responsibilities.
- Assess your institution's readiness for implementing ICS.
- Take the final exam.

| Topic | Making ICS Work! |

Visual 7.3

Visual Description: Making ICS Work!

Instructor Notes

Explain that using ICS at incidents succeeds when everyone assumes personal accountability by:

- **Not going around the chain of command.** Only take direction from your immediate ICS supervisor (might not be your day-to-day supervisor). Exchange of information is encouraged; however, all assignments and resource requests must go through your immediate ICS supervisor.

- **Reporting critical information** about safety hazards, status, changing conditions/needs within assigned areas, and resource needs.

- **Not self-dispatching.** Do not start responding unless you are deployed or your actions are critical for life and safety. Make sure to check in when you begin your assignment. If the plan is not working or your assigned activity cannot be completed, tell your supervisor. Do not create your own plan of action.

| Topic | Recordkeeping and Demobilization |

Visual 7.4

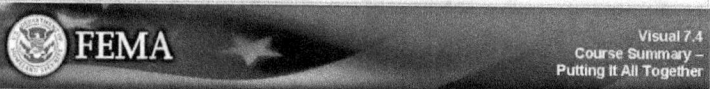

Recordkeeping

- Print or type all entries.
- Enter dates by month/day/year format.
- Enter date and time on all forms and records. Use local time.
- Fill in all blanks. Use N/A as appropriate.
- Use military 24-hour time.

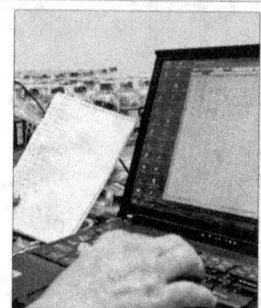

FEMA

Visual 7.4
Course Summary –
Putting It All Together

Visual Description: Recordkeeping

Instructor Notes

All incidents require some form of recordkeeping. Requirements vary depending upon the agencies involved and the nature of the incident. Below are general guidelines for incident recordkeeping:

- Print or type all entries.
- Enter dates by month/day/year format.
- Enter date and time on all forms and records. Use local time.
- Fill in all blanks. Use N/A as appropriate.
- Use military 24-hour time.

| Topic | Recordkeeping and Demobilization |

Visual 7.5

Demobilization

At the end of your assignment:
- Complete all tasks and required forms/reports.
- Brief replacements, subordinates, and supervisor.
- Evaluate the performance of subordinates.
- Follow check-out procedures.
- Return any incident-issued equipment or other nonexpendable supplies.
- Complete post-incident reports, critiques, evaluations, and medical followup.
- Complete all time records or other accounting obligations.

FEMA

Visual 7.5
Course Summary –
Putting It All Together

Visual Description: Demobilization

Instructor Notes

Explain that resource demobilization occurs at the end of your assignment or when the incident is resolved. Before leaving an incident assignment, you should:

- Complete all tasks and required forms/reports.
- Brief replacements, subordinates, and supervisor.
- Evaluate the performance of subordinates.
- Follow check-out procedures.
- Return any incident-issued equipment or other nonexpendable supplies.
- Complete post-incident reports, critiques, evaluations, and medical followup.
- Complete all time records or other accounting obligations.

| Topic | Voices of Experience |

Visual 7.6

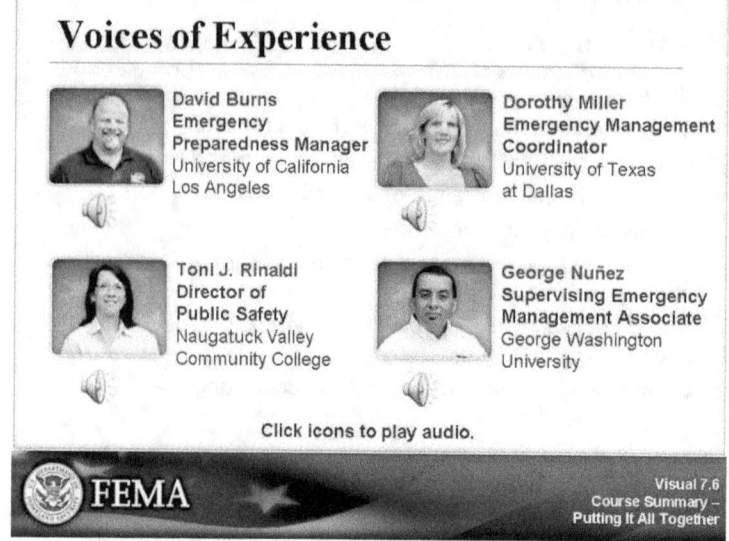

Visual Description: Voices of Experience

Instructor Notes

Tell the participants they will be hearing "voices of experience" from campus personnel about ICS.

Click on each icon to hear the "voice of experience."

Audio Transcripts:

David Burns
Emergency Preparedness Manager
University of California Los Angeles

ICS is a process and one of the important processes is the pre-planning that goes in, the preparedness, the forward thinking – thinking forward as to what might occur so that when an incident does occur, logical steps and sequences can occur.

(Continued on next page.)

Audio Transcripts (Continued):

Toni J. Rinaldi
Director of Public Safety
Naugatuck Valley Community College

There's a lot of steps that help to make ICS work before the actual incident occurs and nowadays particularly you hear a lot about interagency cooperation, mutual aid agreements, memorandums of understanding, and what it all boils down to—it's communication. It's about communication, both within your agency so that people understand what their role is in an incident and that it's not just delegated or relegated to the public safety or first responder section, but it's everyone's responsibility on a college campus to respond to and to have an active role in response to an incident.

Dorothy Miller
Emergency Management Coordinator
University of Texas at Dallas

You entrust people that you know before, if somebody comes on the scene that I have no idea who they are, I don't know if they should be on the scene so I don't what their credentials are. I don't know who they work for, so it creates this little security issue if you don't know who those people are and it's just wasting time. The relationship-building aspect is huge in this field.

George Nuñez
Supervising Emergency Management Associate
George Washington University

Being in the field of emergency management I think it is important that institutions of higher education understand that they need to have comprehensive emergency management plans. By having comprehensive plans that cover all hazards, that cover all response, all entities at the university or college campus, we're able to integrate all of these components into an incident. College or institutions of higher education need to be prepared—that is probably the biggest emphasis or most important thing that college campuses can do is be prepared.

Visual 7.7

Check Plans, Policies, and Regulations

Do preparedness plans, policies, and regulations:

- Comply with NIMS, including ICS?
- Cover all hazards?
- Include delegations of authority (as appropriate)?
- Include up-to-date information?

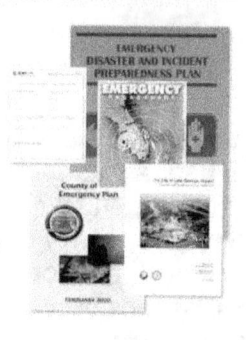

FEMA

Visual 7.7
Course Summary –
Putting It All Together

Visual Description: Check Plans, Policies, and Regulations

Instructor Notes

Note that preparedness plans may take many forms, but the most common include:

- **Emergency Operations Plans (EOPs).**

  Note: EOPs are developed at the Federal, State, tribal, and local levels to provide a uniform response to all hazards that a community may face. EOPs written after October 2005 must be consistent with the National Incident Management System (NIMS).

- **Standard Operating Guidelines (SOGs) and Standard Operating Procedures (SOPs).**

- **Institutional, jurisdictional, or agency policies.**

A jurisdiction's preparedness plans, policies, and regulations must:

✓ Comply with NIMS, including ICS.
✓ Cover all hazards and be based on risk assessments.
✓ Include delegations of authority (as appropriate).
✓ Include up-to-date information about resources available for assignment during a response.
✓ Include contact information for institution administrators and response personnel.

| Topic | Preparedness |

Visual 7.8

Training, Credentialing, and Exercising

- Do you have sufficient qualified personnel to assume ICS Command and key General Staff positions?
- Can you verify that personnel meet established professional standards for:
  - Training?
  - Experience?
  - Performance?
- When was the last tabletop or functional exercise that practiced ICS? Do you use ICS during planned events (e.g., sporting events, commencement)?

FEMA

Visual 7.8
Course Summary –
Putting It All Together

Visual Description: Training, Credentialing, and Exercising

Instructor Notes

Incident responders must be well trained and qualified. As part of the planning process, it is important to consider:

- If there are sufficient qualified personnel to assume ICS Command and General Staff positions.

  Explain that the Executive Policy Group is responsible for ensuring that a qualified Incident Commander has been designated for the incident. Some jurisdictions and institutions maintain a roster of qualified Incident Commanders based on the complexity of the incident.

- If the institution can verify and document that personnel meet established professional standards for:
  - Training.
  - Experience.
  - Performance.

- When the last tabletop or functional exercise was conducted to practice command and coordination functions.

Additional information on training requirements can be found at the National Integration Center Web site: www.fema.gov/emergency/nims

---

> **Tell the participants to take 5 minutes to complete the preparedness questionnaire on the next page. After 5 minutes, ask if any volunteers would like to share their responses to the questionnaire.**

Topic   Preparedness

NIMS/ICS Preparedness Assessment

Instructions: Assess your campus' readiness to implement NIMS/ICS. Read each statement and answer yes or no. For any questions that you answer no, add an action item in the space below.

	Yes	No	Not Sure
Are your emergency operations plan, policies, and procedures consistent with the ICS principles taught in this course?	☐	☐	☐
Do you have the needed communications and other equipment, and vests, badges, and other supplies to implement ICS?	☐	☐	☐
Can responders from different agencies (e.g., fire, police, public works) communicate with institution personnel during an emergency?	☐	☐	☐
Have you identified qualified personnel to assume ICS Command and General Staff positions?	☐	☐	☐
Do you have sufficient backup personnel for all key ICS positions?	☐	☐	☐
Have you identified potential locations for ICS facilities (e.g., Incident Command Post, Staging Area, Base, Camp, Heliports, etc.)?	☐	☐	☐
Do you practice applying ICS during drills and planned events?	☐	☐	☐
Within the past year, have you conducted an exercise for Unified Command with different agencies?	☐	☐	☐
Are after-action reviews conducted to identify lessons learned following exercises, drills, planned events, and incidents?	☐	☐	☐

Use the space below to jot down actions that you must take when you return to your campus and the people that should be involved.

Topic	Preparedness

Visual 7.9

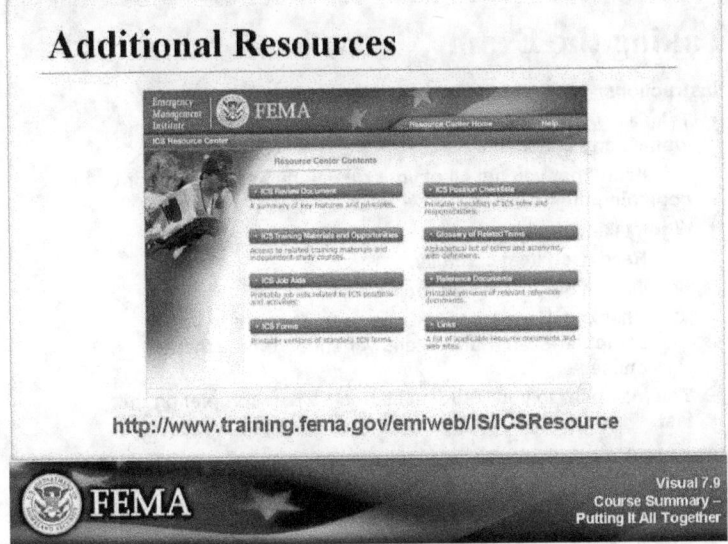

Visual Description: Additional Resources

Instructor Notes

Additional resources can be found at the EMI ICS online resource center. The resource center can be accessed at http://www.training.fema.gov/emiweb/IS/ICSResource.

Ask if anyone has any questions before continuing to the course exam.

Topic	Taking the Exam and Feedback

Visual 7.10

Taking the Exam

Instructions:
- Take a few moments to review your Student Manuals and identify any questions.
- Make sure that you get all of your questions answered prior to beginning the final test.
- When taking the test . . .
  1. Read each item carefully.
  2. Circle your answer on the test.
  3. Check your work and transfer your answers to the computer-scan (bubble) answer sheet or take the test online.
→ You may refer to your Student Manuals when completing this test.

FEMA

Visual 7.10
Course Summary –
Putting It All Together

Visual Description: Taking the Exam

Instructor Notes

Note: Additional guidance appears on the next page.

Present the following ICS 100.HE test instructions:

1. Take a few moments to review your Student Manuals and identify any questions.
2. Make sure that you get all of your questions answered prior to beginning the final test.
3. When taking the test . . .
   - Read each item carefully.
   - Circle your answer on the test.
   - Check your work and transfer your answers to the computer-scan (bubble) answer sheet or take the test online.

Tell the participants that they may refer to their Student Manuals when completing this test.

Important Instructor Note: It is important that you allow the participants enough time to review the course materials prior to taking the exam. If time permits, you can facilitate a structured review of the materials using the following techniques:

- Assign each team a lesson and have them summarize and present the key points to remember.
- Select five to seven of the most critical points from each lesson. Present a brief review of these points. Ask questions to ensure that the participants remember the most important information.

When the review is completed, distribute the exams. Remain in the room to monitor the exam and to be available for questions. Collect the completed exams.

Instructor Note:

To receive a certificate of completion, participants must take the 25-question multiple-choice final exam, submit an answer sheet (to EMI's Independent Study Office), and score 75% on the test. Two options exist for test submission:

Participants submit their tests online, and upon successful completion receive an e-mail message with a link to their electronic certification.

- Go to http://training.fema.gov/IS/crslist.asp and click on the link for ICS-100.HE
- Click on "Take Final Exam."

Instructions for group delivery: Tests can be provided upon request by calling (301) 447-1200. Answer sheets can be requested online at http://training.fema.gov/IS/ansreq.asp.

The completed answer sheets can then be submitted as a group to:

EMI Independent Study
16825 South Seton Ave.
Emmitsburg, MD 21727

| Topic | Taking the Exam and Feedback |

Visual 7.11

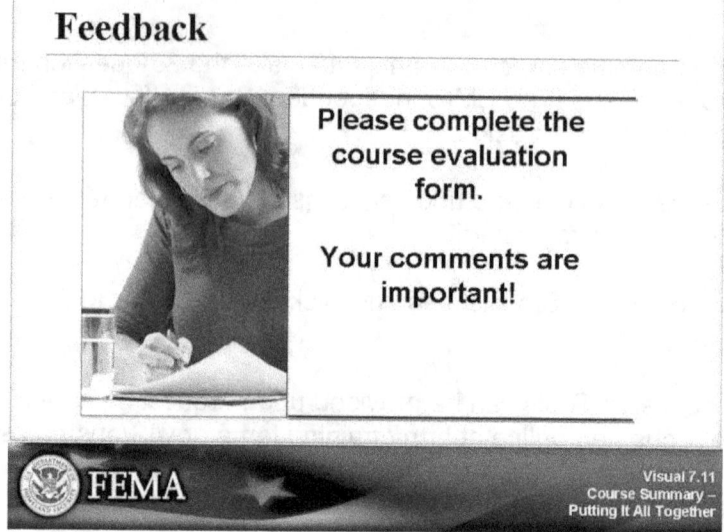

Visual Description: Feedback

Instructor Notes

Emphasize that completing the course evaluation form is important. Participants' comments will be used to evaluate the effectiveness of this course and make changes for future versions. Please use the course evaluation forms provided by the organization sponsoring the course.

www.ingramcontent.com/pod-product-compliance
Lightning Source LLC
Chambersburg PA
CBHW081821280526

45789CB00007B/2293